Social Work in Europe: Educating for Change

Edited by:

Karen Lyons and Sue Lawrence

VENTURE PRESS

© British Association of Social Workers, 2006

BASW website: http://www.basw.co.uk

All rights reserved. No part of this publication may be reproduced, stored in a retrieval system, or transmitted, in any form or by any means, electronic, mechanical, photocopying, recording or otherwise, without the prior permission of Venture Press

Published by
VENTURE PRESS
16 Kent Street
Birmingham
B5 6RD

British Library Cataloguing-in-Publication Data
A catalogue record for this book is available from the British Library

ISBN   1 86178 072 9 (paperback)

Cover and text designed by:
Hobbs the Printers Ltd
Brunel Road
Totton
SO40 3WX

Printed in Great Britain

Contents

Part 1: The European Context

1. Setting the Scene: Social Work and Europe   3

2. A Changing Europe   17

Part 2: Educating for the Social Professions

Part 3: Learning from Experience

List of Figures and Tables

List of Figures

List of Tables

Preface

The past two decades or so have seen significant changes in both social work and education for the social professions in many countries, and also in the construction of Europe. The idea for this book originated in the editors' separate and sometimes combined activities in relation to different aspects of social work education, particularly in the European context. It seemed as if it would be timely to reflect on recent developments in education for the social professions, not so much on a comparative basis (as has recently been done by others) but on a more thematic basis. We therefore invited other contributors to join us in producing a text that hopefully locates thinking and practices in relation to social work education in a European context as well as linking them to wider debates that are current in the social professional field.

Perhaps, as with any edited and many other books, this has been a venture that has proved more time consuming than originally anticipated and it has had a more chequered history than some. The normal 'exigencies of the service' in people's full-time posts sometimes threatened to derail the project completely! Ironically, these included the bringing on stream of the new social work degree in the UK, albeit this was an overdue development that we welcomed, not least to bring us in line with many European counterparts. We are grateful to the chapter authors – both those who stuck with us throughout the project and those who joined at a very late date – for their contributions and hope that the result justifies our various efforts.

There are of course other thanks to be given – to our families for support and forbearance while work (again) invades the domestic scene; to Claire Sandamas for technical assistance with producing the final version for the printers; and to IASSW and BASW for their confidence in commissioning this book and their patience in awaiting an outcome. As is customary, we hope that all information is 'correct at the time of going to press' but accept responsibility for any errors that might have crept in and for our own interpretations and perceptions of events and situations. We trust that the book will provide both information and stimulation for readers, enabling them to engage more fully in debates and activities that promote the development of education for the social professions in the European context.

Karen Lyons, Visiting Professor of International Social Work,
London Metropolitan University

Sue Lawrence, MACESS Course Director,
London Metropolitan University

List of Abbreviations

BA ESW	BA European Social Work
BASW	British Association of Social Workers
CAP	Common Agricultural Policy
CCETSW	Central Council for Education and Training in Social Work
CEE	Central and Eastern Europe
CERTS	Centre Europèen de Ressources pour la Recherche en Travail Social (European Resource Centre for Social Work Research)
CoE	Council of Europe
DAA	Deutscher Akademischer Austauschdienst (German Academic Exchange Service)
EASSW	European Association of Schools of Social Work
EC	European Commission
ECB	European Central Bank
ECJ	European Court of Justice
ECRI	European Commission against Racism and Intolerance
ECSC	European Coal and Steel Community
ECTS	European Credit Transfer System
EEC	European Economic Community
EHEA	European Higher Education Area
ERA	European Research Area
ESM	European Social Model
ESRC	Economic and Social Research Council
EU	European Union
EUA	European Universities Association
EUMC	European Monitoring Centre on Racism and Xenophobia

FESET   Formation d'Educateurs Sociaux Europeens (European Social
            Educators Training)
GSCC   General Social Care Council
GDP   Gross Domestic Product
GSP   Growth and Stability Pact
IASSW   International Association of Schools of Social Work
ICP   Inter-university Co-operation Programme
IFSW   International Federation of Social Workers
MACESS   MA Comparative European Social Studies
NARIC   National Academic Recognition Information Centre
NGO   non-governmental organisation
OECD   Organisation for Economic Co-operation and Development
OMC   Open Method of Coordination
RAE   Research Assessment Exercise
SCIE   Social Care Institute for Excellence
UN   United Nations
UNESCO   United Nations Education, Scientific and Cultural Organisation
UNHCR   United Nations High Commission for Refugees

Notes on the Contributors

Lena Dominelli (PhD, CQSW) is Professor of Social Work and Director of the Centre for International Social and Community Relations at the University of Southampton. She was the President of the International Association of Schools of Social Work (1996–2004) and is now the representative to the United Nations of IASSW, as well as being the Association's representative on the editorial board of the journal, *International Social Work*. In addition to teaching, research and international activities, she has published a wide range of books and articles including, most recently, *Anti-oppressive Social Work Theory and Practice* (Dominelli, 2002, London, Palgrave); *Feminist Social Work Theory and Practice* (Dominelli, 2002, London, Palgrave); *Broadening Horizons: International exchanges in social work* (Dominelli and Thomas Bernard, eds, Aldershot, Ashgate); and *Social Work: Theory and practice for a changing profession* (Dominelli, 2004, Cambridge, Polity Press).

Norman Ginsburg (BA) is Professor of Social Policy at London Metropolitan University. He has published and researched across a diverse range of policy areas, including housing, urban regeneration, racism, globalisation, political economy of welfare and cross-national social policy analysis. He recently directed a project analysing instances of economic and social activity in Inner London that counter and reverse processes of social exclusion and economic inactivity. His publications include *Divisions of Welfare: A critical introduction to comparative social policy* (Ginsburg, 1992, London, Sage Publications). He was one of the founders of the journal *Critical Social Policy* in 1980 and continues as a member of the Editorial Board.

Kieron Hatton (PhD, CQSW) is Senior Lecturer in Social and Community Work at the University of Portsmouth. His main area of work is teaching on, and management of, the BA European Social Work course. He is currently carrying out research into the Roma's experience of social work in the Czech Republic. He has published a number of articles relating to European social work, including ones arising from the focus of his doctoral thesis, 'The dialectics of exclusion and empowerment: an examination of the role of social professionals in Denmark, Ireland the UK' (2001).

Sue Lawrence (MA, CQSW, ILTM) is Principal Lecturer at London Metropolitan University and is one of the course conveners and course directors for the MA Comparative European Social Studies (MACESS) course at Hogeschool Zuyd, Maastricht (in the Netherlands). Her publications include 'Exploring articulation and partnering of social work programmes at the universities of Durban Westville and North London' (with Kasiram, M, Partab, R and Dustin, D) *Social Work / Maaksalike Werk* in Africaans, 2004, vol 40, p 1; and 'European post-graduate education and research: Theorising from course development' (with Richardson, J) in Lyons, K (ed) (2005) *Internationalising Social Work Education: Considerations and developments*, BASW/Venture Press Monograph).

Walter Lorenz (MSc, CQSW) is Professor of Applied Social Science at the Free University of Bolzano, Italy. His main area of work is in relation to European dimensions of social work and intercultural/anti-racist pedagogy. His recent publications include *International Standard Setting of Higher Social Work Education* (2001) Stockholm Studies of Social Work 17, Stockholm, Stockholm University (together with Hessle, S, Payne, M and Zavirsek, D); *Für ein soziales Europa: Ausbilden – Lernen – Handeln in den sozialen Professionen* (2002) Mainz, Logophon Verlag (together with Elsen, S and Friesenhahn, G J); and 'Research as an element in social work's ongoing search for identity', in Lovelock, R, Lyons, K and Powell, J (eds) Reflecting on Social Work: Discipline and rofession (2004), Aldershot, Ashgate.

Karen Lyons (PhD, CQSW) was (until summer 2004) Professor of International Social Work at the University of East London and the course director for the MA International Social Work (with either Community Development or Refugee Studies). She is currently Visiting Professor of International Social Work at the University of Hertford and at London Metropolitan University, from where she edits the journal, *International Social Work*. Recent publications include *Reflecting on Social Work: Discipline and profession* (2004) (co-edited with Lovelock, R and Powell, J) Aldershot, Arena; and 'International perspectives on education for social policy and social work' in Burgess, H and Taylor, I (eds) (2004) *Effective Learning and Teaching in Social Policy and Social Work*, London, Kogan Page/ILT/THES). *International Social Work: Global conditions and local practice* (with Manion, H K and Carlsen, M, Basingstoke, Palgrave) is forthcoming

Part I

The European Context

Chapter 1

Setting the scene: social work and Europe

Karen Lyons and Sue Lawrence

Context and rationale

The increased role and scope of intervention of the European Union (EU) in social affairs since around 1990 has seen a burgeoning of collaborative activity and comparative enquiry by professionals in the broad field of social welfare. Over a similar timescale, changes in the political philosophy of Central and Eastern European states have challenged previous conceptions of regional boundaries and economic arrangements and also increased debate about models of welfare provision; and about the role and preparation of professionals concerned with development and implementation of welfare policies. Notwithstanding (or in the face of) the forces of globalisation, over a wide geographical area, the concept of the European region has been strengthened – relative to national concerns and policies – and has been acknowledged as having implications for welfare professionals, including social workers, as well as for other areas of economic and social policy.

It is in this context that we have seen an increase in European networks concerned with policy initiatives; education for 'social professionals'; and comparative research; as well as cross-national activities in the fields of practice and service developments. One consequence has been the establishment of literature (since the late 1980s) with direct relevance to a group of people included in 'the social professions' (Otto and Lorenz, 1998). To date this literature has mainly focused on the nature and organisation of social work (and related occupational groups) and the issues confronting them, using a comparative approach to information and analysis on a country-by-country basis (for example, Munday, 1989; Shardlow and Payne, 1997; Adams et al., 2000; Hamburger et al., 2004). However, there have also been texts that have treated material on a more thematic basis (Cannan et al., 1992; Lorenz, 1994; Adams et al., 2001). But some of these texts are now becoming dated (or even out of print) and it therefore seems appropriate to offer a new perspective on social work in Europe, taking into account the significant enlargement of the EU from May 2004. This book also takes a more thematic approach to an aspect of the broad field of social work that both reflects and sometimes shapes new challenges and opportunities in policy and practice, namely education for the social professions.

The development of literature has been an outcome of, and a response to, the increased opportunities for academic exchange and course developments, including the establishment of specialist courses concerned with 'Europeanisation' of the social professions themselves. Such exchange – and related opportunities and need for new knowledge – has partly been reflected in the establishment of journals such as *Social Work in Europe* (1994–2003), merged from 2004 with the *European Journal of Social Work*, which was established in 1998, as well as in the activities of organisations such as the European Association of Schools of Social Work (EASSW), the European region of the International Federation of Social Workers (IFSW) and *Formation d'Educateurs Sociaux Europeens* (European Social Educator Training, FESET). There have been some useful seminars and conference papers and accounts (mainly in journals) of specific educational and research programmes, broadly promoting the idea of comparative perspectives and the 'Europeanisation' of social care. However, with the exception of a range of scattered material (monographs, articles, conference proceedings and reports or sections in some of the wider literature); a text about practice learning (Doel and Shardlow, 1996); an American text about the implications of globalisation for social work education (Ramanathan and Link, 1999); and a book describing education in different countries, with some chapters in English and some in German (Hamburger et al., 2004), recent books with a focus on education for the social professions in Europe have been lacking.

Aims and objectives

In this context it is timely to present a more comprehensive and critical assessment of how thinking about Europe and regional policies are influencing developments in education for the social professions and to review the rationale and prospects for continuing developments in this area. This edited text therefore aims to present new and updated material about trends, issues and models in education for the social professions in a European context, including in relation to knowledge creation through research. Differently authored chapters draw on a wide range of personal experience in European research, exchange programmes and joint curriculum developments, as well as on the literature and documentation about the intent and effects of regional policies in the development of education and training programmes for social workers and related occupational groups. The book takes a thematic rather than country-specific approach and draws on examples from across Europe (primarily but not exclusively from the 25 countries now included in the EU), as well as considering the supra-national framework provided through regional bodies and policies. It aims to review some of the literature, to extend thinking about the nature of 'a social Europe' and to explore the implications of this concept for the education of social professionals.

The book's objectives are thus to:

● update and enable ready access to information and ideas currently 'scattered' in a range of publications and sometimes unpublished sources, as well as on websites;
● contribute to the debate about the role and concept of a social Europe as relevant to the education of social professionals;
● identify and analyse specific cross-national or European activities and policies that have impacted on or have implications for education for the social professions;
● reframe and re-examine the familiar educational components, 'knowledge, skills and values', in a European context;
● critically examine assumptions about the nature of education for the social professions and the extent to which harmonisation or convergence and the development of a 'European identity' among social professionals might be desirable or achievable.

While the book might be assumed to be primarily of interest to educators and students, it should also offer something to policy makers and practitioners in the fields of social work, youth and community work, community education and social pedagogy, in Britain and other European countries. Additionally, while it will be of value to students on courses that have already developed a European perspective and/or opportunities for comparative study and inter-cultural learning, current concerns about the growth of social problems that need to be tackled at European rather than only at a national level make it relevant to a much wider readership. More obviously, the book is relevant to anyone anticipating involvement in cross-national research, curriculum development or other educational initiatives in relation to the preparation of practitioners for work in the social professions. However, before proceeding to give further information about the structure and content of the book, it seems appropriate to consider what we might mean by the terms 'social work' and 'social professions' and what is encompassed in 'Europe'.

Defining social work and social professions

Defining social work is a task that has faced social work educators and policy makers in diverse societies, in many cases for more than a century. It is indeed a dynamic and contested term and one that has often been assumed to be essentially a local construct, relevant only to a specific country in a given period. However, there has been increased recognition of the existence of forms of practice (now in most countries of the world) with commonalities in relation to the knowledge, skills and values needed to address social problems, which are also acknowledged to share similarities. Additionally, there has been some evidence of the recognition of the increased interdependence of countries and of problems that transcend national borders and for which common action – at continental if not international level – might be needed (Lyons, 1999a; Healy, 2001). Thus, at the beginning of the 21st century, at a World Congress in Montreal, two of the major associations concerned with representing social work (IFSW and the International Association of Schools of Social Work [IASSW]) agreed a new definition of social work, as follows:

> The social work profession promotes social change, problem solving in human relationships and the empowerment and liberation of people to enhance well-being. Utilising theories of human behaviour and social systems, social work intervenes at the points where people interact with their environments. Principles of human rights and social justice are fundamental to social work. (Source: www.ifsw.org.uk)

This short statement aims to be broad and inclusive and to leave scope for the wide diversity of institutional and educational arrangements characteristic of social work in different countries. It still assumes an occupation that is primarily concerned with identifying and addressing social problems in national or local cultural and environmental contexts, and indeed comparative study of social work in different countries demonstrates how national histories, ideologies and economics have shaped – and continue to influence – the development of social work organisation and practice.

Meanwhile, inclusivity and recognition of the different occupational roles and titles found in the professional field were also in evidence in a specifically European context, from the 1990s. Arising from the collaboration of personnel from educational projects crossing various disciplinary and occupational as well as national boundaries, the term, 'social professions' came into use from about 1996. It was perhaps first formally suggested at the concluding conference related to the evaluation of the impact of Erasmus projects in the social work and allied fields, such as youth and community work, social pedagogy and animation (Seibel and Lorenz, 1998) as well as being given further exposure in the first editorial of the new journal, *European Journal of Social Work* (Otto and Lorenz, 1998). While the contributors to this book have generally used the term 'social work', this should be taken as a broad field for which the term 'social professions' would often be more appropriate.

When considering the role and scope of social work, particularly in an international context, it is important to acknowledge that the 'social' that we work within is a dynamic form that changes in dimension and direction over time, as well as regionally, nationally and internationally, as is the case with the 'social' in social policy (Lewis, 2000). Any definition of the focus of the 'social' is merely a 'snapshot' of the relationship between the economic and political view of the priorities with which social work should be concerned at any one time and in any one place, albeit linked to its historical traditions, which help to form and shape the nature of that concern. The 'social', then, indicates the priorities of a particular society and set of social relationships at an historical moment and will be rooted in the traditional relationships and perceived problems that that society views as a threat to its solidarity or order. The 'social' in this sense will therefore give different priorities, agendas and ways of practising to social workers in different places and at different times.

At a supranational level, the 'social' is increasingly becoming the concern of the EU and this impacts upon member states by giving priority to various issues through a number of measures. For instance, at the time of writing, EU social policy is particularly concerned with employment, inclusion and old age pensions although 'hard law' in the area of social policy to the year 2004, amounted to only 10 Directives around maternity and parental leave and discrimination of various kinds in relation to aspects of employment and social policy.

Despite differences in terminology and in the boundaries of different forms of social work across European countries, and the often significant differences in the education and training traditions associated with particular 'branches' of social work, it has been documented that historically social work in Europe has much in common (Lorenz, 1994). It has also been possible to analyse social work as organised within the statutory, voluntary, private and informal sectors and to relate these to the broader context of welfare regimes (Lorenz 1994). Furthermore, as identified above, the values underpinning social work are now being articulated in international terms (www.ifsw.org), and in a professional sense, these act, alongside international and national codes of practice, as a filter and a guide in how policies are implemented by social workers. Therefore, although the 'social' space defined for social work in Europe varies from country to country (and sometimes from region to region), the similarities of the profession are such that common themes and trends have been found worthy of analysis and/or comparison, as have been the diversities. In addition, the impact of policy initiatives of supranational organisations, including the EU and the Council of Europe (CoE), provide rich territory for cross-national implications to be explored. However, before this task can begin, the term 'Europe' also deserves some consideration.

Locating Europe

In this book, 'Europe' is used as a principal point of reference, although as a key term it has only provisional and unstable meanings (Fink et al., 2001). Social work commentators have adopted a variety of approaches over the past decade or so in defining Europe, concentrating either on the countries in the EU at that time (Adams et al., 2000; Cannan et al., 1992) or defining Europe as 'not a fixed entity' but a 'project' with no clear geographical boundaries (Lorenz, 1994, p 1) or as socially constructed, containing the possibility of many different constructions (Pringle, 1998).

Europe can therefore be seen to be a contested construct – it has not had, and still lacks, a singular identity. Historically, the term 'Christendom' was applied to a number of 'countries' spreading North and West from the Middle East into what we now call Europe but the boundaries were frequently challenged by other civilisations and religious traditions from North Africa and the East. While some countries became established as nation states relatively early (for example the UK became a politically unified state in the 18th century), it was not until the late 19th century that other countries assumed the names and forms more familiar today (for example, Italy) and the integrity of political and linguistic borders was an issue for many countries, particularly in Central and Eastern Europe, for most of the 20th century. Additionally, there have continued to be challenges to the national boundaries and identity of particular countries, as illustrated in the (for some still unresolved) case of Ireland, or in the recent (1990s) break-up of 'Yugoslavia'.

Thus, even an attempt at defining Europe geographically as a continent has problems: its spatial boundaries have historically shifted to the North, South, East and West, including and excluding different nation states over time. It is also currently defined differently by different organisations, importantly, for our purposes, the EU (increasing from 15 to 25 members states since 1 May 2004) but also extending to the CoE. The latter was established in 1949 and (at the time of writing) comprises 46 members (www.coe.int). Its importance lies in the role it has played in formulating conventions related to human and social rights, the ongoing role of the European Court of Human Rights, and its role as a moral and cultural force rather than having political and economic responsibilities. However, the notion of Europe is also important, if differently constituted, in sporting and cultural terms by organisations such as the European Football Association or the Eurovision Song Contest. Some of the ways in which the EU in particular has sought to define and promote both a social Europe and Europe as an entity having cultural characteristics will be discussed later in this section.

Meanwhile, it may be useful to recap on the way in which Europe, as now represented in the form of the EU, has evolved since the second half of the 20th century (see also Chapter 2). This entity has undergone changes in membership, geographical spread, goals and name since its origins from the European Coal and Steel Community (ECSC). The ECSC was established in 1951 by the Paris Treaty, with goals related to both economic reconstruction (after the Second World War) and peacekeeping. The six signatories (Belgium, France, Germany, Italy, Luxembourg and the Netherlands) later signed the Treaty of Rome (1957) to establish the European Economic Community (EEC). Membership was extended by the addition of new countries in 1972 (Denmark, Ireland and the UK), again in the 1980s (Greece, Spain and Portugal) and also in the 1990s (Austria, Finland and Sweden) (Cannan et al., 1992; Hantrais, 1995). While the focus and range of influence shifted during the 1970s and 1980s (to include a more 'social' component), new directions were partly signified in the Treaty of Maastricht (1992) and the change in title to the European Union (EU). It was to this body that 10 more countries successfully gained entry in 2004 (Cyprus, Malta, Estonia, Latvia, Lithuania, Poland, Hungary, the Czech Republic, Slovakia and Slovenia) and other countries (including Turkey and Croatia) are currently working to meet the democratic (including human rights) and economic conditions required for membership of this European 'club'.

Even leaving aside the issue of actual membership, the EU has a contested form, with pressures and disagreement arising both internally and externally. Membership, inclusion and exclusion are fiercely debated and its direction is unsettled in terms of its collective identity and purpose (Clarke, 2001). There are currently a number of easily identifiable internal divisions within the EU. One such example is 'Euroland', comprising those member states that have adopted the euro as a common currency, but at the time of writing, covering only 12 of the 25 states in membership. Another example is the group of countries covered by the Schengen Agreement. This allows free movement of people between adjoining member states but to date only 10 of the 25 member states have signed this agreement and a guiding principle of the Maastricht Treaty – namely free movement of labour (as well as of capital, goods and services) within the EU – is not a realistic or possible choice for many.

The EU also has less clearly defined boundaries of inclusion and exclusion based on broad areas of commonality and difference, providing another form of identity. For example, the (post-) industrial North and West (previously with the exception of Ireland) can be contrasted with the less industrially developed South (now including the islands of Cyprus and Malta in addition to Greece, Italy, Spain and Portugal) and also the accession countries to the East (the eight Central and Eastern European countries of the Former Soviet Union) stretching from the Baltic (Estonia) in the North to the Mediterranean (Slovenia) in the South. While such boundaries can partly be drawn on economic and rural/urban lines, they also reflect, to some extent, different religious traditions as well.

It can be noted here that, as currently constituted, the EU still reflects, to some extent, the predominantly Christian heritage of its member states, not withstanding denominational distinctions arising from major schisms between the Orthodox, Catholic and Protestant traditions. However, apart from the longstanding existence of Jewish minorities in many countries, significant numbers of people within EU borders now adhere to the Muslim and other faiths, reflecting the colonial histories and other reasons for population mobility and resettlement that have characterised particular national histories as well as more recent events and processes, such as globalisation. It is true that all member states are formally secular, politically, and also in terms of the beliefs and practices of more or less people in national populations. However, the existence of different religious faiths is also related, in many countries, to the existence of minority ethnic groups with different racial and cultural characteristics and the recognition of multiculturalism has posed challenges both within nation states and to those wishing to promote a sense of European identity and a common culture.

Turning briefly to the notion of culture, Clarke describes national culture as 'a composite or compound *formation*, not a simple unity' but having 'distinctions within a unity'. The 'unity' that is a national culture is made up of many diverse elements that are 'interconnected ... but not reducible to one another' (Clarke, 2004, p. 36; emphasis in original). The 'unity in difference' that goes to make up national culture has unifying elements described as 'articulated ensembles' pointing to the 'constructed and contestable character of cultural formations' (Clark, 2004, p. 38). The construction of a national culture can thus be seen as a complex subject of analysis – how much more complex then is the task of building a culture spanning a number of nations.

Despite this, the task of building a distinctive European identity is observable in some actions of the EU, most notably through moves to establish economic integration, but also through developing a distinctive social policy profile and through efforts to promote notions of European civilisation and cultural identity. In the first instance, economic integration has been central to the European Project and has culminated in the establishment of the European Central Bank and the introduction of the euro. The Central Bank is now responsible for setting pan-European interest rates and overseeing the Growth and Stability Pact between member states. In the second instance, the development of a distinctive social policy profile of relatively extensive welfare states has sometimes been described as the European Social Model (ESM). The EU itself has advanced modest transnational European social rights and programmes, sometimes referred to as 'Social Europe'.

Europeanness has also been linked to notions of a European 'civilisation', which in turn was closely related to national examples of colonisation; and, as mentioned above, this legacy persists in the presence of descendants of formerly colonised peoples within many EU states. It can also be seen in the continuing and increasing gap between European and poorer African and Asian countries, reinforcing the racialised dimension of 'Fortress Europe'. Finally, the EU has been creating cultural forms, symbols and practices, following the Single European Act of 1986, in an attempt to build a sense of European cultural identity – 'an imagined unity of people, place and ways of life' (Clarke, 2004, p. 36). These take the form of 'top-down' symbols and 'bottom-up' processes and projects. (These four aspects of 'Europeanisation' are further explored in Chapter 2).

So how well developed is the project to promote a distinctly European identity or sense of belonging to Europe for the peoples of the EU? The EU parliamentary elections of June 2004 would suggest that this project has far to go, with under half (45.5%) of the population in member states of EU25 considering it worthwhile to vote. This is a significant downward trend in turnout, considering that in 1979, 63% of European citizens voted (Elections, 2004). However, it must be acknowledged that a whole variety of factors influence voting behaviour and turnout, so this, while interesting, may not in itself be an indicator of more or less identity or commitment to the EU. And how relevant to social professionals are some of the particular themes apparent in current EU projects and challenges? Areas of particular relevance to social workers and their educational and research concerns form the substance of later chapters, and are mentioned below in a summary of the structure and content of this book.

Structure and content of this book: a preview

The book is organised into three parts with a concluding discussion. *Part 1: 'Setting the Scene: Social Work and Europe'* (Chapters 1 and 2) provides a brief overview of the European context: it analyses the development of policies and systems at regional level that have 'driven' the Europeanisation of welfare developments and specifically of education for the social professions. *Part 2: 'Educating for the Social Professions'* (Chapters 3–5) explores three key components of educational systems and provisions for the social professions. The issues identified relate to theoretical paradigms and curricula in relation to professional boundaries; the role of research (including comparative research) in professional education; and the rationale for developing anti-racist programmes in the light of increased recognition of cultural and ethnic diversity and the development of local and regional policies aimed at combating racism, discrimination and social exclusion. *Part 3: 'Learning from Experience'* (Chapters 6 and 7 together with the concluding chapter, Chapter 8) presents an analysis of particular initiatives in the areas of undergraduate provision, and postgraduate developments; considers how these might inform future developments; and identifies emerging challenges and opportunities for the social professions and those concerned with social professionals' education.

In terms of individual chapters, in Chapter 2, 'A Changing Europe', Ginsburg and Lawrence explore the impact of changes in the geography and politics of Europe (the EU and the former Soviet block) on social policy and welfare in the latter part of the 20th and early 21st century (Hantrais, 1995; Leibfried and Pierson, 1995; Ginsburg, 1996). It has been increasingly recognised that although the main focus of the EU is economic, that agenda cannot, in the long term, be pursued without some attention to the social and cultural spheres. So, for instance, the European Commission (the executive arm of the EU), in recognition of this, has a culture department that funds arts, heritage and language projects, as well as its growing commitment to a 'social Europe', one of the themes explored in Chapter 2. Major trends and developments in ideological views of welfare and their impact on the delivery of services, arising from both sides of the political spectrum are identified. Specific policies and programmes in relation to higher education and the social services that have prompted comparative research and/or joint educational initiatives are analysed and a critical overview is presented of Erasmus, Tempus, Socrates and other recent and current programmes/funding arrangements relevant to the 'Europeanisation' of education and research for the social professions.

In Chapter 3, 'Education for the Social Professions', Lorenz considers the goals of social professional education and compares different models of training and educational approaches across Europe. He presents an analysis of social pedagogy and other traditions relative to (British) assumptions about social work, and about the knowledge, skills and value bases utilised and promoted by education and training programmes. Further, he considers such questions as 'How far is "harmonisation" of training a desirable or achievable goal?' and 'On what basis might a new paradigm be formulated to inform the development of social work and its concomitant educational programmes?'.

Assuming research to be a related aspect of social work education and a cornerstone for developing knowledge and theory for practice, Lyons in Chapter 4, 'Research and Professional Education', explores the extent to which research is seen as a necessary part of education for the social professions in a range of European countries. The chapter includes an analysis of the implications of the location, length and level of training for research activity among social work (and related) educators and students, as well as the effects of funding and policy decisions for the development of cross-national or European-wide research and evaluation programmes. The particular characteristics, challenges and opportunities associated with carrying out research within a comparative framework or from a European perspective are also considered.

In Chapter 5, 'Racialised Identities: New Challenges for Social Work Education', Dominelli examines the shifting nature of 'race' and racialised identities in Western Europe. She argues that racism is practised at personal, institutional and cultural levels, including as evidenced by the growth in popularity of far-right parties in a number of European countries and their presence in the European Parliament itself. Dominelli examines different strategies for avoiding or addressing racism and identifies the growth of anti-racist initiatives by both the EU and the CoE, including through programmes involving young people. Dominelli makes the case for the development of anti-racist social work by social professionals and suggests that this approach offers more scope for addressing racism than other strategies, such as multicultural, intercultural or culturally competent social work. Finally, she draws on previous experience of running anti-racist courses to identify the components needed if social work education is to prepare students for anti-racist practice.

Turning to Part 3: 'Learning from Experience', the EU has seen the education agenda as one of its most important and successful projects in the context of building Europeanness, as well as being crucial to human capital formation (to ensure its competitiveness in global trade and economics) and the implications of the European education agenda for the social professions are explored in Chapters 6 and 7. Hatton in Chapter 6, 'Europe and the Undergraduate Programme', reflects on dilemmas and possibilities of developing joint curricula and common awards at the undergraduate level. The extent to which the European dimension can be part of a professional training programme or an academic 'add-on' varies between countries. Such differences can be related to differing assumptions about pedagogy and assessment, as well as issues in relation to field placements and projects. Lessons are drawn particularly from an Anglo-Danish programme.

In Chapter 7, 'Postgraduate Provision in Europe', Lawrence gives some examples of comparative trends in relation to post-qualifying opportunities and expectations in Europe, and considers how postgraduate programmes have interpreted the 'European dimension' and what makes such programmes 'European'. Drawing on the Maastricht–London Metropolitan University programme and other examples, Lawrence discusses the contribution of joint academic programmes to the development of research-minded European practitioners. Structural aspects, such as validation arrangements for joint programmes, are explored in the light of their role in pushing curriculum development forward. Consideration is also given to the employment outcomes for graduates, and how such qualifications are being received in different countries.

Finally, the book concludes with some consideration of new challenges for the broad field of social work and implications for professional education. Thus, in Chapter 8, 'Imagining the Future', Lyons and Lawrence explore how current and emerging social trends might suggest a continuing place for the development of European dimensions and cross-national initiatives in education and research, particularly in a context where globalisation is a buzz word and the need to promote European education within a wider international context is being recognised at the policy level. As well as identifying social issues associated with increased interdependence, we identify labour mobility among social professionals themselves as both reflecting more general patterns of temporary or permanent migration and contributing to a more diverse workforce. This trend has implications for social work education and affords new opportunities to develop cross-national activities and contribute to the development of European policies in the social field.

Chapter 2

A Changing Europe

Norman Ginsburg and Sue Lawrence

Introduction

Changes in the geopolitical and economic profile of Europe over the second half of the 20th century have had a major impact on the way social policy and welfare are both conceptualised and delivered. In this chapter we will be discussing some of the key trends and developments, and the discourses that have both prompted and resulted from these changes. First, we outline developments in European geopolitics, particularly the European Union (EU). Then we examine briefly a range of socioeconomic forces that have shaped individual welfare states over recent decades, before considering the nature of Europeanisation as one of these forces. The social policy dimensions of the European Social Model and of Social Europe are then considered. Finally, some of the education policies and programmes of the EU and other European institutions are examined as a particularly relevant policy field for the social professions.

Western Europe has seen an increasing political, social and economic integration of its constituent nation states over the past 25 years. With the collapse of the Soviet block in the late 1980s, the integration processes are now embracing Central and Eastern Europe (CEE). The extent and depth of the integration is much debated and discussed, and it is easy either to exaggerate or to underestimate. European integration is a classic example of a glass, both half full and half empty. Even the definition of what is meant by 'Europe' as a political and economic entity is much debated. In Western Europe, the term is often used to describe the member states of the EU as constituted in 1995 (15 states) and expanded in 2004 (25 states). Another intuitive approach referred to the 'core states' of (Western) Europe as being the EU15 plus Norway and Switzerland, which have both rejected EU membership via referendums. Quite separate from the EU and a much less prominent institution of 'official Europe' is the Council of Europe (CoE) with its 45 member states, including Russia and Turkey. As mentioned in Chapter 1, the CoE is predominantly a human rights organisation, its most prominent institution being the European Court of Human Rights in Strasbourg. Here we will focus predominantly although not exclusively on changes in the EU.

The gestation of the EU is usually traced to 1950 when the French foreign minister proposed what amounted to an industrial and, hence, political partnership with the newly created Federal Republic of (West) Germany. Policy making in the EU is built around a series of international treaties, the first of which, the Treaty of Rome (1957), founded the EU, or as it was then called, the European Economic Community (EEC). The six founder members were France, West Germany, Italy, the Netherlands, Belgium and Luxembourg. In 1973, Denmark, Ireland and the UK joined, followed by Greece in 1981, Spain and Portugal in 1986, and Austria, Finland and Sweden in 1995. The greatest enlargement of all took place in 2004 with the 'accession' of the Czech Republic, Hungary, Poland, Slovenia, Slovakia, Latvia, Lithuania, Estonia, Malta and Cyprus. The population of the EU had thus grown from around 160 million in 1957 to about 450 million by 2004. The EU has a complex web of constituent bodies, the most powerful being the Council of Ministers, which brings together the member state governments. Under the remit of the Council, the European Commission (EC) in Brussels (the EU's civil service) develops policy proposals and organises policy implementation, which is regulated by the European Court of Justice (ECJ). The European Parliament is potentially the democratic arm of the EU but many view it largely as a talking shop and question its relevance and power. The European Central Bank (ECB) is the EU's central financial institution, governing the euro and monetary policy.

The EU describes itself as 'a family of democratic European countries', which is neither a federal state (as yet) nor just another international organisation. The member states 'delegate some of their sovereignty ... on specific matters of joint interest' ('The European Union at a glance': www.europa.eu.int). The origins of the EU lie in the (re)construction of liberal democratic capitalism in North Western Europe after the Second World War. As Milward (2002, p. 16) puts it, 'the European construction remains a peace treaty based on a rejection of the politics of 1933-45' and, equally, also of Soviet-style political economy in the Cold War context. In many ways these political aims have now been achieved, with the apparently permanent eradication of fascist government in Spain, Portugal and Greece, and the more recent advent of liberal democratic capitalism in CEE. Hence, for example, in 2000, as an immediate reaction to the participation of the neo-fascist Haider and his party in Austria's government, the EU inaugurated a diplomatic boycott of Austria that was rescinded after a few months. Certainly the growth of far-right, racist and xenophobic politics across the continent in recent years shows that liberal democracy is never entirely secure in Europe. The considerable limits to political integration are illustrated, above all perhaps, by the very limited development of coherent European foreign and defence policies. Europe's disarray in the face of the break-up of Yugoslavia, and more recently, the invasion of Iraq, suggests that 'after forty years of assertions of the need for a common European defence policy, nothing has changed' (Milward, 2002, p. 26).

The biggest change in Europe's geopolitics since 1989 is obviously the abandonment of Soviet-style communism in favour of capitalism (of a more or less liberal-democratic hue) in CEE. This led to the reunification of Germany and the 2004 enlargement of the EU. The impact of such a momentous shift will be felt for many decades to come. The fact that Europeans now more or less share a political and economic 'system' in common for the first time is a hugely significant aspect of Europeanisation, however great the differences in economic development and political culture across the nation states. This is not just a geopolitical change in terms of big government and big business. Its effects are felt by everyone, not least in the movement of people across old boundaries, the creation of 'new' nation states, and the new inequalities in CEE.

Changes in welfare ideology and delivery in Europe

Reorientation and restructuring of the Western European welfare states have been mapped onto and coincided with many other processes aside from Europeanisation. These include economic globalisation, the rise of neo-liberalism as the global economic orthodoxy, the decline of collectivist social democracy and socialism, the shift from direct government by state bodies to governance by regulation of civil society (for example, privatisation), the re-emergence of mass unemployment in the 1980s for the first time since World War Two, the increasing burden of care work (low paid and unpaid) falling particularly on women, the consolidation of rich Western states as multicultural and multi-ethnic societies, and the reassertion of 'old' ethnicities as a basis for political power (commonly associated in North Western Europe with the growth of the racist far right). It is often impossible to specify what can be considered to be a feature of Europeanisation rather than one of these other processes, particularly economic globalisation and the rise of neo-liberalism. Europeanisation itself can, of course, be construed as a clear instance of globalisation, conceived as the creation of an economic block to compete globally on level terms with, for example, the North American Free Trade Association (NAFTA), and as an emerging, supranational political structure, potentially eclipsing the nation state.

It is problematic to assess the impact of even one of the change processes mentioned above on the welfare state for one country, so attempting to do it for the whole continent must be prefaced by a 'health warning' about the particularity of welfare states. Welfare states are in many ways unique constructions in each country, and their development is shaped, above all perhaps, by 'path dependencies'. In other words, the path followed by policy change is shaped by the historical and institutional context of a particular society, and, once established, tends to stay in place, keeping reform within the boundaries of the path. Europe now consists of over 50 nation states, which have experienced the changing geopolitical and economic environment in very diverse ways. Here, therefore, we are confined to a brief review of some of the common threads identified by analysts.

Based on an overview of the impact of economic globalisation, Prior and Sykes (2001, pp. 199–200) found that 'significant changes have, indeed, occurred in European welfare states ... related to [economic] globalization', particularly in three aspects: unemployed 'activation policies' to improve 'employability'; 'marketization' of welfare services; and 'cost cutting' in social spending (Taylor-Gooby, 2001, has similar findings for seven Western European states). In the Nordic and Bismarckian states these changes amounted only to 'retrenchment' and adjustment to the more competitive economic environment. In the UK, France and the Netherlands, the changes were more fundamental and more aptly described as 'restructuring'. The situation in CEE is obviously an even deeper and more fundamental transformation, which is very much still in process. While also responding to these pressures, the EU's cohesion states (Ireland, Greece, Spain and Portugal) have also been 'catching up' with the North Western European welfare model.

Activation

Western European states have all developed their active labour market policies in response to mass unemployment, the accompanying growth of benefits spending and, in some cases, labour shortages. Measures take essentially three forms: 'human capital development' involves high-cost, high-skill employment training; 'labour force attachment' or 'workfare' involves getting people into low-wage, less-skilled jobs, supported by tax credits and employer subsidies; and benefit 'push' measures involve the withdrawal or reduction of benefits for unemployed people. In many states too, policy has sometimes encouraged the deactivation of older workers in the attempt to bring down the unemployment figures, for example through adjustment of pensions and incapacity benefits rules to facilitate early retirement. Labour market deactivation has, of course, been rampant in CEE, using meagre early retirement and disability pensions as a means of cushioning (Müller, 2002).

Marketisation

The clearest examples of marketisation have been in CEE where the World Bank and the International Monetary Fund (IMF) have actively sought establishment of as much privatised welfare as politically possible, particularly in the field of old age pensions (Müller, 2002). In Western Europe, a major impetus for marketisation came from the Thatcher regime in the UK in the 1980s, including the subsidised sale of social rented housing to tenants, incentives to shift to private personal pensions, the 'contracting out' of elements of public services to private contractors (for example, school meals, hospital cleaning, domiciliary and residential care of the elderly). Since 1997 under the Blair government, the emphasis has been on the transfer of public services to non-profit, third sector bodies, alongside the development of new forms of corporate, for-profit involvement in the welfare state (for example, provision of non-clinical services in new hospitals). The involvement of private, non-profit organisations in welfare is, of course, nothing new, particularly in the Bismarckian and Southern European states. However, the drive towards more commercial privatisations of pensions and welfare services is becoming stronger as egalitarian, universalistic principles of tax-funded public sector provision give way to the individualistic, consumerist principles of the so-called competitive market economy.

Cost cutting

Cross-national data for Western European states in the period 1984-97 indicated either an increased or a static level of social expenditure as measured by the Organization for Economic Co-operation and

Development (OECD), with the exception of two previously high-spending states (Belgium and the Netherlands) where there has been a significant reduction (Castles, 2001). Social expenditure here includes pensions and cash benefits, as well as health and social care services financed by the state, but does not include education or law and order. However, governments have used all kinds of rationing, efficiency and managerial measures to contain the further growth of social expenditure. From the viewpoint of the pensioner and benefit claimant in many states, the past two decades have seen a decline in their incomes relative to others, as income inequality and salary dispersion have increased markedly in many states. Equally, the demand for health and social care services has increased, and the costs of providing them have increased relative to general costs in the economy. Hence there is a widespread and accurate perception of a retrenchment of the welfare state, despite the cold economic data that suggest stability. In CEE in the early 1990s it was the production and consumer subsidies on energy, housing and food that were cut right back, while social expenditure was to some extent maintained (Deacon, 2000). The cuts in basic subsidies, the closure of many state enterprises and ensuing unemployment, and the dramatic increase in wage and salary dispersion were naturally experienced by many as a severe deterioration in the welfare state.

The development of Europeanisation

In Western Europe, the biggest change in the shape of Europeanisation has been the developing economic integration of the EU. This has been a continuing process since it was revitalised in the early 1980s by President Mitterand of France and Chancellor Kohl of West Germany as a means of digging Western Europe out of recession. As Milward (2002, p. 19) says, 'The common market is still the cement of the EU, the one institution of European integration which meets the US on equal terms and in whose negotiations with the outside world each member state can pursue a national advantage which otherwise would be hard to win'. Thus far, of course, economic integration has culminated in the establishment of the euro, behind which lies the ECB, which sets pan-euroland interest rates and oversees the Growth and Stability Pact (GSP). The GSP amounts to a number of monetary policy rules, which limit governments' borrowing and long-term debt with the aim of achieving a low and convergent level of inflation across the EU. It has been argued that the ECB and the GSP are the Trojan horses of neo-liberal economic policy within the EU. Certainly the rigidity of the GSP has proved to be very problematic, with France and Germany, among others, ignoring its strictures in the early years of the 21st century in their efforts to revive economic growth through government borrowing. Nevertheless the fact that the peoples of 12 Western European states use the same currency is in itself perhaps a small but significant cultural shift towards Europeanisation. The euro is a bold experiment, and its long-term success is only likely to be secured if other aspects of economic integration are developed, particularly in the realms of taxation and public spending.

Beyond matters of commerce, the Treaty of Rome (1957) envisaged 'an ever closer union among the peoples of Europe' ('Treaty of Rome: Preamble: www.hri.org/docs/Rome57). In the wake of the Single European Act (1986), which set in train the so-called single market, the EC suggested in 1988 that 'the world of culture clearly cannot remain outside the process of completion of the big European internal market: that process demands the formation of a true European culture area' (quoted by Shore, 2000, p. 15). This gets to the heart of the EU's problematic – it is essentially an economic partnership; hence, perhaps, its most symbolic achievement to date is the inauguration of the euro. But can you have a successful, long-term economic union without political, social and cultural integration? The EC thinks not, and hence has a culture department that funds arts, heritage and language projects. Higher education has been a particularly significant arena of EU 'cultural' intervention, discussed in more detail in the final section of this chapter.

In the late 1980s the EC inaugurated cultural symbols in an effort to market and popularise the EU – hence the EU flag and anthem (Beethoven's Ode to Joy). The latter perhaps symbolises an elite or intellectual view of European culture, as derived from the Roman and Greek civilisations, Judaeo-Christian theology, the Renaissance and the Enlightenment. Profoundly significant as these traditions are, they seem unlikely to provide a sufficiently modern, popular cultural basis for contemporary European identity. Alongside the momentum for economic integration, the most popular rationale for the EU is the drive for peace (and liberal democracy) in Europe. However, language, historical memories and myths of ethnic descent continue to divide Europeans, while economic and political modernisation pushes them together. Eurobarometer, the EU's public opinion survey, consistently demonstrates that 'in most EU countries only a very small percentage of people (around 5%) declare having an exclusive European identity while up to 50 per cent do not have any sense of European identity ... [and] that European political identity is weak and there is great variation across states' (Llobera, 2001, p. 173). Such data lead Shore (2000, p. 19) to conclude that 'the peoples of Europe have simply not embraced the European idea'. This is particularly so perhaps in terms of popular perceptions of the top-down, technocratic output from the EC in Brussels.

Yet there is also a 'surreptitious' or 'bottom-up' Europeanisation taking place, as discussed, for example, by Leonard (1998). Examples include the success of the European Champions League in soccer, big infrastructural projects such as the Channel Tunnel and the bridge linking Denmark and Sweden, the growth of cultural tourism, the emergence of 'modern European cuisine' in states without much of a national cuisine, and the acquisition of second homes in other member states. Thus Llobera (2001) suggests that European identity is in the process of construction. Shore (2000, p. 228), however, argues that most of the above processes are linked to globalisation rather than Europeanisation, and reminds us that there is a danger of confusing 'patterns of consumption with processes of identity formation'.

Conceptions of Europeanness have also, and perhaps still are in many quarters, linked to notions of the superiority of European 'civilisation' or, alternatively, to its inherent and essential difference to other civilisations. European 'civilisation' is indissolubly linked with European colonialism, which as Hansen (2004) reminds us is by no means entirely extinct. Until recent decades, 'Europeans' in the eyes of most of the rest of the world were experienced as white colonisers. Inevitably this legacy continues to loom large, not least in the presence of descendants of formerly colonised peoples within most EU states, but also in the economic chasm between rich (European) and poor (Asian and African) states. The term 'Fortress Europe' emerged in the late 1980s to describe renewed Western European efforts to exclude 'Others', particularly from Africa and Asia. Even before the most recent wave of anti-Islamism and xeno-racism, the danger was clearly that, as Delanty (1995, p. 155) suggested, 'European identity is rapidly becoming a white, bourgeois populism defined in opposition to the Muslim world and the Third World'. In the wake of the attacks in the US in September 2001 ('9/11') this must appear to many non-Europeans to have become a pre-eminent aspect of Europeanness.

Yet such racialised, exclusionary elements in Europeanness are surely unsustainable, not simply in moral terms, but also economically and socially. Europe will need migrants from poor countries and most Western European states are already multi-ethnic, multicultural formations, whose social cohesion cannot be secured on the basis of the white, Judaeo-Christian, and colonial inheritances from the past. In terms of formal status, Delanty (2000, p. 121) and others argue that European citizenship based on residence rather than birth should become 'a means of enfranchising immigrants ... complementing rather than undermining national citizenship'. Two prominent European social thinkers made a passionate call for a common EU foreign policy in the wake of the invasion of Iraq, suggesting that 'the recognition of differences – the mutual recognition of the Other ... – can also become the mark of a common [European] identity' (Habermas and Derrida, 2003, p. 294). Taking this further, Amin (2003, p. 3) suggests that an appropriate 'philosophical ethos' should be one that 'publicizes empathy and engagement with the stranger as the essence of what it is to be 'European'. However, the question of whether a multicultural, multi-ethnic conception of Europeanness can or should be mapped out is problematic, because it inevitably suggests something particular about Europe in a context in which transnational identity, citizenship and culture are developing on a global scale (see Gustafson, 2002, pp. 464–5). As Young (2003, p. 2) points out, 'the call to embrace a particularist European identity ... means constructing anew the distinction between insiders and outsiders', between a club of rich Western societies and the others to the East and South.

Certainly one widely recognised aspect of Europeanness is its distinctive social policy profile. There are two sides to this. First, Western European states have, on the whole, developed more extensive and expensive welfare states than the rich countries outside Europe, which is sometimes described as the European Social Model (ESM). Second, the EU itself has had a modest but significant impact in advancing and developing transnational, European social rights and social programmes, increasingly reaching into areas of the state and civil society beyond the industrial/economic sphere, sometimes dubbed Social Europe. Here we discuss each of these in turn.

The European social model or models

The ESM emerged as a concept in the 1980s, as a new phase in European integration was developing around the idea of a 'single market'. It suggests a guarantee by governments to protect workers and their families from fundamental risks in the capitalist market economy, including the developing European single market, such as loss of income due to old age, unemployment, sickness and disability, alongside provision of adequate education, employment training, health care, social care and housing services. This commitment is made in exchange for industrial harmony and commitment to public–private partnership in economic management. Although much of this was more or less a reality in North Western Europe, it was much less so in Southern

Europe. The ESM discourse revisits the consensual notion of the 'social market economy' associated with post-war Christian Democracy in Germany, and endorsed by conservative governments in other member states. Jacques Delors, EC President from 1985 to 1993, as a social democrat envisaged the ESM as somewhat more collectivist and egalitarian as, in the words of Ross (1995, p. 46), 'a humane social order based upon the mixed economy, civilized industrial relations, the welfare state, and a commitment to basic social justice'. The contemporary ESM is thus an amalgam of Christian democratic and social democratic social and economic policy as practised throughout most of North Western Europe in the post-war decades. The ESM cannot be dismissed as empty rhetoric. The states of North Western Europe devote a significantly higher proportion of their economic resources to public social expenditure than others. Out of 29 OECD states in 1998, 10 of the top 12 welfare state spenders were in the EU15, the others being Switzerland and Norway (OECD, 2002). Of 21 OECD states in the mid-1990s, the top 10 in terms of low-income poverty were eight EU15 states plus the Czech Republic and Hungary. In terms of this particular measure of social justice, the ESM as a whole certainly does not come out particularly well, with major states like the UK, Germany and Italy having higher levels of income poverty than Australia and Japan (Förster and Pearson, 2002, Fig 1, p. 13).

The notion of the ESM as a single model cannot, of course, be taken too far. Remember the health warning above, regarding path dependency. Esping-Andersen (1990) famously identified three contrasting worlds of welfare capitalism, judged in terms of the extent and adequacy of their social protection measures. The social democratic, conservative (Christian democratic) and liberal models were all more or less distinguishable within the pre-2004 EU15, as well as a possible fourth model, the Southern European. So, to say the least, the ESM embraces a considerable diversity of welfare regimes, although no doubt Delors would baulk at the liberal and Southern European regimes being included in the ESM. In respect of Southern Europe, it must be noted that Portugal, Spain and Greece have rapidly moved towards the ESM since becoming EU members. Consideration of Britain and Ireland as liberal regimes, perhaps outside the ESM, is a matter of debate.

Social Europe

The reality of Social Europe in terms of actual social policy is very limited and likely to remain so. There is no reason to believe that a European welfare state is in the making (Kleinman, 2002). In the core areas of social policy (benefits and pensions, education, health, housing, and social care) the impact and role of the EU has been small. In the early decades of the EU there was a discourse of harmonisation and convergence in social policy, seen largely as a by-product of economic market integration. The gathering pace of economic integration since the mid-1980s has been accompanied by a considerably greater volume of social policy discourse at the EU level, but the reality has been a strengthening of the principle of subsidiarity alongside intergovernmental policy coordination where appropriate. Subsidiarity suggests that policy making and implementation should take place at the most local possible level, recognising the family as the basic institution for social welfare. This Christian democratic principle (with its roots in Catholic thinking, Cannan et al., 1992) came to the forefront in the 1990s in the context of the emergence of 'a Europe of the Regions', and as a bulwark against lingering social democratic, socialist aspirations for a more centralised Social Europe. Besides the principle of subsidiarity, there are two other reasons for the severely limited development of Social Europe. First, national politicians and civil servants, the nation state itself, derive a great deal of their legitimacy from the provision of social policy. Such responsibilities are jealously guarded, and interventions from Brussels would be neither popular nor practical. Second, the neo-liberal consensus that guides economic integration is fundamentally at odds with the welfare state, and, with its anti-inflationary, monetarist zeal, is intent on reducing social expenditure and cutting back the tentacles of the welfare state. Despite these severe constraints, Social Europe does have a distinctive existence both as the discourse already alluded to, and in concrete policy forms, including social spending programmes, social rights legislation and regulation, and policy coordination processes. We will examine each of these briefly.

In 2000 the EU budget was €93.3 billion, which is just 1.1% of the aggregate Gross Domestic Product (GDP) of the EU states, while public spending as a whole averages about 45% of GDP. The vast majority of the budget is devoted to 'economic' spheres, including the Common Agricultural Policy (CAP), supporting farmers, and Structural Funds investing in environmental and infrastructural projects. Much of this investment is, of course, involved in protecting and generating employment, including support for job training programmes, and therefore constitutes social policy. In earlier decades the EU funded modest anti-poverty programmes, but a proposed further programme in 1998 was rejected by the Council of Ministers.

Perhaps the greatest impact of Social Europe has been in the development of legislation in the few areas of social policy in which the EC has been given some 'competence'. EU Directives on health and safety at work, women's employment rights, parental leave, working time, workers' rights on transfer of company ownership, and industrial democracy have had a considerable, positive impact on employment rights, especially in the more backward states such as the UK. This has spilt over into issues going well beyond the workplace such as child care, sexual harassment, privatisation, work–life balance, and the rights of separated/divorced partners. There is an emergent 'single market in health care', which is beginning to be tested in terms of health care 'tourism' and transnational EU rights to health care. Threlfall (2002, 2003) calls such developments 'incipient social integration'. The European Court of Justice (ECJ) oversees the enforcement of Directives and has now made more than 300 decisions on social policy. Only competition policy takes up more of its work (Kleinman, 2002).

A major leap forward in EU social legislation took place in 2000 with the passage of the Race Equality Directive and the Employment Discrimination Directive. The former, also known as Article 13 of the Amsterdam Treaty (1997), aspires to prohibit direct and indirect discrimination on grounds of ethnicity and 'race' across the public services and most of civil society. It requires member state governments to have anti-discrimination agencies to support and monitor implementation. Article 13 should have been incorporated into national legislation by summer 2003, but no member states had completed the process by the deadline. 'Many member states have resisted implementing it, [and] have compromised its effectiveness' (der Boghossian, 2003), so a protracted struggle continues on this. The Employment Discrimination Directive seeks to outlaw workplace discrimination on grounds of religion, sexual orientation, age and disability. It is being phased in over the period to 2006, but successful implementation will be a lengthy and difficult process.

The EC has used several strategies in trying to maintain the Social Europe momentum in recent years, particularly in relation to the unemployment problem. The Green Paper (EC, 1993) and the White Paper (EC, 1994) on European social policy argued for EU social policy as an essential part of the drive for economic competitiveness, advocating a shift from cash benefits for unemployed people to more investment in employment-related education and training, that is, active labour market policies or workfare. In 2000 the EC came up with a new means of trying to deliver on such aspirations, called the Open Method of Coordination (OMC), sometimes referred to as the Lisbon process after the summit where it was adopted. The process requires member governments to produce annual, national action plans on issues like unemployment and social inclusion, which are scrutinised by the EC, which then develops recommendations and benchmarks with a view to coordinating measures across the member states. Hence national governments are 'required to focus on jointly defined problems and policy objectives.... By exposing their actual performance to comparative benchmarking on the basis of agreed indicators, to peer review and to public scrutiny, the process does in fact provide favourable conditions for 'learning by monitoring' (Scharpf, 2002, p. 654). It is far too early in the process to know whether this aspiration is realistic.

One area of social policy where increased EU coordination and harmonisation has occurred is immigration. In 1997 the Schengen Agreement introduced harmonised border control and visa policies for 13 of the EU15 member states, backed by a powerful information system. The Amsterdam Treaty (1997) envisages that asylum and immigration policy will eventually be the responsibility of the EU rather than of the member states. This is a dramatic shift from the notion that this area of policy is an essential element in national sovereignty and the idea of the nation state; this was regarded as sacrosanct, especially by British governments until very recently. Ironically the British government is now pressing for more effective EU measures to stem the flow of asylum applications. As Toynbee (2002) notes, 'However much the EU thinks itself under siege, it takes very few of the world's 20 million displaced people, most of them grouped at the borders of the poorest countries. The US, Canada, Australia and others take in tens of thousands of UNHCR- [United Nations High Commissioner for Refugees-] registered refugees, but the EU will not as yet take any but those who arrive here under their own steam'. At the 1999 EU Council meeting in Tampere (Finland),

> the main elements of a common EU asylum and immigration policy were agreed [including]
>
> ● Partnership with countries of origin and transit to promote human and political rights.
> ● A common European asylum system based on the full and inclusive application of the Geneva Convention.
> ● A more vigorous integration policy to ensure fair treatment.
> ● The management of migration flows, with an emphasis on secure external borders and fighting crime'. (Düvell and Jordan, 2002, pp 505–6)

The last element perhaps elevates the idea of Fortress Europe to a more official level. Progress towards implementing these measures has been slow (Lavenex, 2001; Boswell, 2002) because member state governments have been reluctant to give up to Brussels their power to control immigration, particularly with the heightened anti-asylum seeker feeling and the electoral success of anti-immigration, nationalistic far-right parties in the early 2000s. However, the EU's Seville Summit in summer 2002 marked a further strengthening of Fortress Europe. Britain and Spain wanted to make development aid to poor countries dependent on cooperation over the return of asylum seekers. While this was rejected, the EU now reserves the right to take sanctions against uncooperative states over asylum seekers. At Seville it was also agreed to experiment with EU border policing in the Mediterranean and on the eastern border.

In 2000 Geddes suggested that the Fortress has several perimeter walls. The EU15 constituted an inner sanctum; outside this are the 'accession states', whose workers will (in a managed way) fill the gaps in the labour market in the inner sanctum; the third layer are the 'transit' countries from where some limited, managed migration will be permitted, but where United Nations (UN)/EU-managed camps of 'undeserving' asylum seekers/economic migrants are being set up; finally, right outside the fortress will be people from the 'excluded' states of Asia (beyond Eurasia) and Africa. The racialised dimension of the stratification is obvious (see also Chapter 5).

EU education policies

Education, alongside the other fields of social policy, has become an increasingly significant arena for European intervention, driven by very much the same cultural, social and economic concerns that drive national education policies. We have already touched on the EU's keenness to promote the European cultural dimension. The liberal democratic consensus envisages education as a key vehicle for the transmission of a shared culture (European, national and regional) and thus for the development of a sense of European citizenship. Education is also an important dimension of the problem of social exclusion in the EU. Low educational attainment has been identified by Tsakloglou and Papadopoulos (2002) as one of five key factors associated with increased risk of social exclusion or 'chronic cumulative disadvantage' in the EU. The aspiration for closer cooperation between member states at all levels of education led to the adoption of the first Education Action Programme in 1976 with objectives of harmonising the recognition of qualifications and periods of study, information exchange and improved mobility for students, researchers and teachers (Milner, 1998).

However, the key driver of the development of European education policy is the 'economic' dimension. In the narrowest sense this has focused on the finance and development of employment training, which can be traced right back to the Treaty of Rome. The Maastricht Treaty of 1992 obliges the EC to implement vocational training measures, but only permits the EU to 'contribute to the development of quality education' (Murphy, 2003, p. 556), which is purposely vague. The boundary between vocational training and other forms of education is, of course, impossible to delineate precisely, and it is this ambiguity that has informed the emergence of the 'educational space' within the EU. Here we will concentrate on vocational and higher education, as the field of education policy that has figured most prominently in EU discourse. Education in schools remains more firmly within the competence of the member states alone.

With the emergence of Social Europe in the 1980s, the EU markedly increased its activity in the education sphere, most notably with the development of programmes of educational cooperation such as Erasmus (see below). This was legitimated in terms of a discourse suggesting the critical importance of educational investment in raising the productivity and competitiveness of the European economy. Investment in 'human capital' through education and vocational training has therefore assumed a much higher profile in the EU discourse in the past two decades (Nóvoa, 2001; Room, 2002). The growing recognition of the importance of education in realising the European project as a whole has been seen principally in terms of its capacity to equip the labour force with the professional and technical competence to compete in the world market and further the goal of economic integration. The development of a 'single market' suggests the free movement of people and, hence, shared understandings and recognition of educational systems and qualifications to facilitate the mobility and exchange of labour, skills and knowledge. Running counter to such aspirations, is, of course the notion that education is central to the particular, national cultures of each member state. The EU has therefore found some difficulty in defining the 'educational space' it can inhabit, for without elements of harmonisation, there can be little meaningful exchange and cooperation between the diverse educational systems of the member states. The actions and initiatives that have flowed from Brussels to facilitate educational exchange and integration are briefly outlined below.

Socrates

Socrates is the European education programme, established in 1995, currently with 31 states taking part – the EU25, the three European Economic Area countries (Iceland, Liechtenstein and Norway) and the three candidate countries (Bulgaria, Romania and Turkey) (EC, 2005). Within Socrates there are several action programmes. The *Comenius* action programme supports secondary school partnerships and in its first five years, 10,000 schools took part. Funded activities have included information and materials exchange, cooperation over curriculum topics, and teacher and pupil exchange. The *Minerva* action programme focuses on open and distance learning, multimedia and the use of information and communication technology. *Lingua* supports projects that encourage language learning. *Grundtvig* is concerned with adult education and lifelong learning. *Eurydice* is an information network providing comparable information on national education systems and policies in Europe. *Arion* supports multilateral study visits for decision makers and senior managers in educational institutions. The *Jean Monnet project* offers subsidies for the establishment of Jean Monnet Chairs, courses and modules in European law, European economy, political studies of European construction and the history of European integration.

Finally, perhaps the best-known action programme is *Erasmus*, launched in 1987 to enable higher education students to study for up to one year in another state, with the time spent studying abroad recognised within their home degree, and more recently through the European Credit Transfer Scheme (ECTS – see below). By October 2002 the total number of Erasmus students reached one million, with around 10,000 undergraduates participating each year and an EU target of three million mobile students by 2010. Academic staff can also access some financial support for mobility under the Erasmus programme. In the original programme, funding was provided for 'Inter-university Co-operation Programmes' (ICPs) and 'networks' of higher education institutions were established and began cooperating on a subject basis. Curriculum development projects, intensive programmes, research projects and other innovative schemes resulted from these academic networks (Lorenz and Seibel, 1998). In 1996 Socrates bi-lateral contracts between universities and higher education institutions were introduced, replacing the ICP network structure and at the time of writing, individual staff exchange is only part-funded by Erasmus, enabling academics to teach for short periods in a partner institution.

Vocational training

The *Leonardo da Vinci programme* began in 1995 and funds a range of international partnerships to improve quality, foster innovation and promote a European dimension in vocational training. The *European Centre for the*

Development of Vocational Training (CEDEFOP) contributes to the development of vocational training through academic and technical activities. The *European Training Foundation* works in non-EU states, supporting the reform and modernisation of their vocational education systems. The EC also has an action plan called *eLearning: Designing Tomorrow's Education*, to help speed up the deployment of a quality infrastructure at a reasonable cost, to step up training and overall digital literacy and to strengthen cooperation and links between all those involved, from schools and training colleges to equipment and service providers.

Cooperation with third countries

The EU places importance on cooperation with countries outside the EU in the field of education and has agreements with the US and Canada. The Tempus programme played an important part in the integration of the EU accession states by funding the establishment of academic networks to exchange information and promote staff and student mobility and helping to establish common practices in administrative and financial accounting systems in higher education in the 2004 accession states. Tempus now covers the former Soviet Union, the Western Balkans and Mongolia, and aims to help modernise higher education in those areas. The *Alfa* and *Alban* are cooperation programmes involving Latin American countries and *Asia-Link* similarly involves many countries in Asia.

Recognition of accreditation

The EU has several initiatives to encourage the transfer of qualifications and experience for academic and professional purposes. The network of National Academic Recognition Information Centres (NARICs) provides advice and information on the academic recognition of diplomas and periods of study undertaken abroad. Other instruments include the Europe Credit Transfer System (ECTS) introduced in 1989 as a common basis for recognising students' study periods abroad through a system of academic credit. Similar initiatives are being set up for vocational training. A network of National Reference Points for vocational qualifications is being set up in the member states. The Commission has recommended a common European format for curricula vitae, and the 'Europass' provides a voluntary means of recording periods of work-linked training outside one's home country.

Through such measures the EU has already succeeded in creating 'a single higher education area' for students. European Union students have to be treated equally in terms of access, fees and accreditation of qualifications. The upshot is something much more differentiated and exciting than convergence could produce, a form of 'social integration' that 'brings wider choice to degree-seekers and greater diversity of individual pathways to the qualifications sought' (Threlfall, 2003, p. 131).

The future

In the EU, as Edwards and Boreham (2003, p. 407) note, 'since the mid 1990s there has been a river of consultation papers, statements, green and white papers, directives, legislation and . memoranda, all ostensibly seeking to promote a learning society through the development of a culture of lifelong learning'. According to Murphy (2003, p. 557) lifelong learning 'has become the educational focus of the EU'. In practice, concepts such as 'a learning society' and 'lifelong learning' are open to differing interpretations, but for the EC they are principally driven by the mission to improve industrial and commercial competitiveness. Hence in March 2000 the Council of Ministers established the ambitious aim that the EU 'must become the most competitive and dynamic knowledge-based economy in the world capable of sustainable economic growth with more and better jobs and greater social cohesion' (Europa, 2005a). It went on to say that '... by 2010, Europe should be the world leader in terms of the quality of its education and training systems' (Europa, 2005b). Difficult questions about whether the promotion of 'high-tech' education and training does generate social cohesion are left aside (Edwards and Boreham, 2003).

The EC's aims for facilitating a learning society and a culture of lifelong learning are to be achieved through a 10-year programme, implemented through the Open Method of Coordination (see above). Planning is underway within the EC to formulate a new generation of programmes by 2007, in response to the very different levels of educational provision in the newly enlarged Europe of 25 member states. There are likely to be three programmes replacing the existing structure: a new *Erasmus Mundus* programme to enhance the quality of higher education and to promote European higher education through cooperation with non-EU states; an *integrated programme in lifelong learning'* – the successor to Socrates and Leonardo programmes, which are to be integrated into one scheme; and *Tempus Plus*, the successor to Tempus.

The Bologna Declaration

Apart from the EU, the CoE has furthered its human rights agenda through educational measures such as its youth work programme. It has opened Youth Centres in Strasbourg and Budapest to train youth workers and young people on topics such as human rights and combating racism and xenophobia. The CoE has been a key player in furthering the recognition of qualifications internationally and is one of the partner organisations in the 'Bologna Process' (see also Chapter 3). In the 1999 Bologna Declaration, the European ministers of education agreed to establish 'a coherent, compatible and competitive European Higher Education Area (EHEA) by 2010' (Europa, 2005a). The agreement seeks to establish:

- a common pattern that distinguishes undergraduate and postgraduate courses;
- systems of credit and credit transfer;
- diploma supplements that make every qualification 'readable' in other parts of the EHEA;
- a structure for quality assurance;
- specific European features (for example, joint degrees, integrated programmes of training and research, promotion of the European dimension in higher education);
- promotion of mobility;
- promotion of the attractiveness of the EHEA.

The diploma supplement has already been developed by the EC, the CoE and the United Nations Education, Scientific and Cultural Organisation (UNESCO) as a product of the Bologna Process. It includes a graduate's personal achievement (transcript) and a description of the national higher education system of their country. It is being adopted by the states included in the Bologna agreement to facilitate educational mobility and exchange, by making qualifications and courses of study transparent and academic credit transferable.

Conclusion

In this chapter, we have considered the substantive yet limited development of Social Europe in recent years. The processes of European economic integration underpinning deeper EU involvement in social policy are balanced by the commitment to the principle of subsidiarity and welfare state sovereignty among the member states. Hence the European Social Model continues to embrace a range of regime types with the broad objective of sustaining social cohesion to ensure stability and growth. Certainly Europe's commitment to a strong welfare state continues to constitute a vital aspect of 'Europeanness'. The various education policies and programmes suggest that governments, non-governmental organisations and intergovernmental bodies regard public education systems as being a dynamic and essential element in generating economic growth and social cohesion.

Education and training for the social professions in Europe is situated mainly in the tertiary or higher education sector of each state education system. The social professions have actively participated in nearly all the appropriate European educational initiatives and programmes. This is remarkable in view of the diversity of social professional traditions and practices, not least their education and training programmes that have always struggled for academic status and respect (Lorenz and Seibel, 1999).

Part 2

Education for the Social Professions

Chapter 3

Education for the Social Professions

Walter Lorenz

Introduction

As indicated in Chapter 2, social work was one of the earliest and most active disciplines seeking European exchanges through the Erasmus and Socrates Programmes (Lorenz et al., 1998). This means that a great deal has been learned about the nature of the different training traditions, curricula and course structures of social work in Europe and that this professional field has been able to establish itself afresh as internationally oriented. There had been two major previous waves of internationalisation that had indelibly shaped the profession. The first was associated with the origins of organised training programmes when the pioneers, through their roots in the international women's and peace movements but also in the context of a scientific interest in comparative approaches to welfare, had promoted the series of international conferences characteristic of the 1920s and early 1930s, until Nazism and the Second World War broke up these efforts (Hering and Waaldkjk, 2003). The second was heralded by the efforts of the United Nations (UN) and the Western Allies to make the development of professional approaches to social, community and group work one of the priorities of post-war social and political reconstruction – both in a Europe ravaged by Fascism and in the Third World, where the process of de-colonialisation was gathering momentum (Altmeyer, 1955). This meant that lecturers and potential 'multipliers' of training were either given the opportunity to train in the US with the help of various aid programmes, or that US and UK experts would set up training centres and courses in Europe to disseminate what were considered key methods in democratic social service delivery (Lorenz, 1994).

This second wave, in particular, was responsible for the widespread impression that social work in all countries conformed to a unified epistemology and in fact formed a coherent, science-based discipline independent of specific cultural presentations. This impression was underlined by the dissemination of US social work textbooks in most European countries accompanied by the rising recognition of the title of 'social worker' in its various linguistic translations and the expectation that this would displace the confusing plethora of pre-existing titles and strengthen the unity of the field. However, the 1960s and 1970s saw instead attempts at 'indigenisation' of social work or at least a rediscovery and affirmation of lines of professional and academic continuity evident before the second wave of internationalisation. In this process, the 'case work dominance' was criticised from two principal positions. The political critique objected to the implied individualism of the method and its overall effect of taking the task of personal adjustment as the point of least resistance in the face of prevailing structural poverty and exclusion. This prompted the establishment of 'radical social work' and the 'rediscovery' of community work approaches, which drew on experiences of local and national campaigns and activists. The 'cultural critique' targeted the 'colour-blindness' of the case work approach and its incapacity to articulate identities in collective and solidarity-constituting ways. The universality of the case work method was therefore challenged from this side by approaches constructed around collective identities such as 'feminist social work' and 'black social work' with their transversal lines of analysis of social problems and of modes of intervention. The net effect was a greater diversification of courses and curricula in the context of which alternative traditions to that of 'social work' once more gained greater significance.

Social pedagogy

One such challenge to the 'social work consensus' came from the field of social pedagogy, an academic tradition closely associated with the development of academic conceptualisations of training needs of social service personnel in Germany but which, on closer inspection, turns out to represent a much more widespread theory paradigm found in countries such as France, Italy, Lithuania, Poland, Spain and Sweden. There is also no reason, for instance, not to subsume the tradition of youth work training in the UK under the family of disciplines constituting 'social pedagogy' as well those of care workers and 'special educators' and the more recent (continental-European) phenomenon of 'animators'. The difference is that social pedagogy as an academic discipline with a long and well-established university tradition is not defined from distinct areas of practice (such as 'youth and community work' or 'residential care work') but from a core epistemological paradigm, which allows for the application of its general concepts in a variety of practice settings, not limited to particular institutions or user groups. In this sense, social work, despite its affinity to sociology, has no comparable disciplinary or conceptual base and has to be constructed in an interdisciplinary way. However, the feature that distinguishes the academic discipline of pedagogy from that of social work most clearly is its affirmation of a 'normal state of society' in which the need for continuous learning and adjustment processes in individuals and institutions is accepted and fostered, for the purpose of enhancing the capacity of individuals, communities and societies at large to solve and prevent social problems. Compared to that societal concept, social work tends to limit its attention to situations and moments where 'deficits' have already become apparent (despite a sometimes rhetorical emphasis on prevention), meaning that large sectors of the population and periods of 'normal life' exist perfectly well without the need for social work intervention. Pedagogy signifies an explicit reflection on all learning processes in which the acquisition of formalised items and competences makes up just a small segment of endeavours, normally associated with the education system and particularly schools. Social pedagogy focuses on the territory beyond the education system, on formal and informal places and occasions where learning takes place and which people utilise, not necessarily because of a deficit, but as a normal part of socialisation and of adjusting to changing societal conditions. Hence in many countries a strong and independent tradition of social pedagogy developed early in the 20th century within university departments of educational sciences, such as in Germany, Poland (Lepalczyk and Marynowicz-Hetka, 2001) and Bulgaria (Vladinska, 2001).

The historical development of social pedagogy in Germany has paradigmatic significance for the complexity of relationships between training and social policy traditions in the social professions in Europe and therefore needs to be briefly summarised. The concept of social pedagogy was shaped in Germany through the confluence of two trends. The transition to conditions of modernity and hence of the division of labour, of complex social relations and of uncertain cultural identities had necessitated an entirely new and more fundamental process of reflection on the scope and method of education to safeguard cultural continuity, social coherence and economic 'progress'. At the same time, the danger of social tensions, civil unrest and widespread need and poverty were recognised more specifically and discussed under the title of 'the social question'. Social pedagogy, as intended by one of the earliest users of the term, Karl Mager in 1844 (cited in Kronen, 1886), applies educational concepts to concrete social and historical contexts and reflects therefore on the totality of the prevailing social conditions and relations (Kronen, 1986). The problems associated with industrialisation were not perceived merely as economic difficulties but as a cultural crisis, and this not only at the level of scholarly analysis but also in terms of social movements, like the German youth movement, which sought to bring about a cultural and social renewal through self-directed educational and social initiatives such hiking, camping and celebrating youthfulness, idealism and friendship. Inevitably, in the course of the actual implementation of training for social pedagogues in this tradition, the meaning of the concept also tended to be defined from the various institutionalised fields of application, as happened with social work, but this counter-move, in the case of social pedagogy, set off a stronger dialectic between deductive and inductive epistemologies (Hamburger, 2003). It heralded a 'pedagogical century' (Rauschenbach, 1999) and pedagogical reform zeal characterised particularly by the Weimar Republic era, only to be stymied by economic constraints and colonised ideologically by Nazism (Sünker and Otto, 1997). Thus the paradigm took some time to re-establish itself in post-war Germany, which it did through the seminal work of Mollenhauer and Thiersch (Niemeyer, 1998).

With the intensification of educational encounters and cooperation facilitated by the various European Union (EU) programmes since the late 1980s (see Chapter 2) the degree of diversification that characterises the field of the social professions in Europe became fully apparent. Training in the social professions had proliferated and, apart from the factor of paradigmatic indigenisation, the differentiation of professional identities within the field was compounded at the institutional level by the dualism between courses based at universities and those operating in the non-university sector. At university level the social professions usually had to be 'accommodated' by established academic disciplines such as social sciences, psychology or pedagogy according to patterns that were not even consistent within the same country and therefore gave rise to many misunderstandings in cross-national comparisons. The non-university sector shows more flexibility in this regard on account of its vocational orientation so that academic disciplines and categories do not confine the development of authentic, practice-related professional identities. But here the discrepancies in social policy structures account for further divergences. For instance, the low status of youth policy in the context of

British social policy renders youth work training almost 'invisible' as a distinct entity within the social professions whereas, in countries such as France, Germany or Italy, youth policies confirm the broad but distinct professional 'family' of educators and pedagogues (Köhnen, 1992).

In terms of the remit of the EU this diversity constituted a problem to be resolved by means of closer cooperation and coordination, associated with the promise of thereby enhancing the status of a professional field that was still struggling to rid itself of the image of a 'semi-profession'. The selection by the European Commission (EC) of social work as one of the disciplines to be awarded the distinction of forming a 'Thematic Network' under the Erasmus Programme in 1996 reflected this intention, seen as opportune by the EC particularly in the light of the importance attributed to social services and the corresponding training of professional personnel in the post-communist countries of Central and Eastern Europe (CEE), which, according to the EC, were to be given the chance of commencing right away with a more 'modern' and unified training pattern. The analyses conducted by the first Thematic Network for the Social Professions (ECSPRESS) and the experiences of its working parties clearly refuted the suitability of a harmonisation and unification agenda for this professional field (Lorenz and Seibel, 1999).

Instead, ECSPRESS undertook a painstaking process of examining the meaning and value of the existing diversity of training patterns, professional titles and practice traditions against the background of cultural patterns in social policy and in recognition of the historical nature of the requisite professional methodology (Lorenz and Seibel, 1998). The members of the Thematic Network concluded that a decisive element of a common identity lay in the recognition of such a multidimensional diversity not as the result of mere historical contingencies, never 'corrected' by scientific and methodological stringency, but as a means of engaging with the individual and collective determinants of identity in the context of which social problems and issues manifest themselves and need to be respected in all forms of intervention. The diversity of professional and theoretical reference points appears therefore neither as a preliminary condition of professionalisation to be overcome nor as an unquestionable cultural 'fact' to be preserved with essentialising justifications. Rather, this diversity becomes an heuristic challenge for the development of a transnational and (in the present context) European discourse on the social professions, which proceeds in a critical comparative manner to determine educational requirements that are relevant to specific cultural and social policy contexts and are at the same time subject to scientific, transnational scrutiny (Lorenz, 1999). Professional titles and qualifications, seen in this light, are socially constructed symbols whose meaning has to be interpreted in specific communicative contexts rather than taken as absolute reference points for the identification of particular methodologies and practice fields.

Analysing diversity

The diversity in question presents itself along different comparative axes that intersect and influence each other to some extent. One such axis describes the relationship between professional practice and training and stretches from one pole, where practice is regarded as the 'outcome' of theoretical analysis and hypothesis-testing methodology, to the other, where training counts as supplementary to forms of practice that are primarily experience-based, integrated and only partly amenable to scientific analysis and classification. While there was traditionally an assumption that social professional fields that require a continuity of contacts with service users such as care work or work in nurseries and youth centres belonged to the latter end of this polarity and therapeutic activities occupied the other, theory-centred end of the spectrum, this pattern has never been consistent in all countries and in any case is shifting and breaking up into much finer nuances as the relationship of theory to practice is becoming ever more problematic. What is important to consider, however, is that all fields of the social professions are caught up in this polarity and that what at first glance appears to be a universal pattern (such as the preponderance cited) on closer inspection reveals numerous inconsistencies and tensions that cannot be systematised.

This is related to a second axis, which characterises the variety of meanings attached to different third-level institutions. Superficially, universities are associated with being the reserve of 'pure theoretical endeavour' where applicability of knowledge thereby produced to particular practice fields is only of secondary importance, whereas other third-level institutions such as polytechnics, Fachhochschulen in Germany and Austria, and other technological and vocational training institutions derive their legitimation from producing knowledge that is immediately applicable to specific settings. It would be logical on the grounds of the applied nature of the social professions to assume therefore that training started and is predominantly located in the non-university third-level institutions. This is, however, not necessarily the case and the relationship between both types of educational institutions is therefore much more complex. First, training for social work did commence (for instance in the cases of Finland, Iceland, Ireland and the UK) at the university level, and second, there are significant variations in the understanding of the role of a university where disciplines such as medicine, law and indeed pedagogy have a firmly established place everywhere as applied disciplines. Profound shifts can be observed along this axis in international comparisons in as much as wholesale reclassifications have taken place. For instance, in the UK, polytechnics became universities virtually overnight and in Germany, *Fachhochschulen* adopted the official English translation of their title as 'universities of applied sciences'. Formally, it is therefore justified to confirm the trend towards the 'academisation' of training in the European social professions and particularly in social work, first noted in the pioneering comparative work by Brauns and Kramer in 1986. Where two decades ago Finland, Iceland and Ireland were the only countries in Europe where social work training was located exclusively at the university level, this is now also the case in Estonia, Italy, Latvia, Lithuania, the UK and, depending on terminology, in Germany, Norway, Sweden and Spain, with most other countries having a dual system. It has to be asked, however, whether the nature of training has been changed thereby or whether the changes reflect a change in the nature of universities and their role in society – a question that can only be answered against the background of a detailed analysis of the conditions prevailing in particular countries.

Italy might serve as a case example here. Successive governmental decrees sought to introduce greater uniformity and higher standards in the plethora of schools of social work that had existed until the 1990s by first forcing these schools to become affiliated to university departments and then abolishing them entirely, permitting only university degrees as valid social work qualifications (Dal Pra Ponticelli, 2001). This meant, on the one hand, a considerable gain in professional and public status for social work and a victory for the Italian professional social work association (which had long advocated a university degree as the qualifying standard). On the other hand, this was a hollow victory since hardly any of the professionally experienced and qualified tutors running and teaching the previous schools managed to find entry to highly protected university chairs or become heads of departments. Their expertise was either lost entirely to the new curricula or tapped only through limited teaching contracts while the 'established' university disciplines such as sociology and psychology now determine the nature of social work training.

The third axis concerns the nature of social policy in the different European countries. The social professions have a highly ambivalent relationship with a state's social policies. On the one hand, welfare and its organisation is clearly determined (directly and indirectly) by the general orientation of national social policy, by the laws that allow or prescribe interventions of a material and professional kind, even where they do not necessarily mention any one of the social professions explicitly. On the other hand, it has been part of the development of professional autonomy in the entire field to create a distance from the possibility, perceived as a danger, of becoming ancillary to the welfare system and of turning professionals into bureaucratic executors of welfare policies. Two strategies were pursued, particularly by social work, in order to avoid this incorporation. One was the strong emphasis on international links, which were regarded as a means of emancipating the profession from a national state of dependency and creating a methodological discourse that could form a corrective to procedures determined by bureaucratic regulations. The other was the introduction of academic training, which was expressly multidisciplinary and, in most training traditions, not in-service and agency based, so as to allow for a considerable degree of independent reflection and the growth of an autonomous methodology. Nevertheless, social policy frameworks determine the nature of the relationship between professional and service user in as much as social professionals are on the whole not free agents but belong to governmental or non-governmental welfare organisations, which, through their organisational structure and ideological orientation, have a bearing on the definition of social problems and hence on the different frameworks of problem resolution and the meaning of social solidarity.

The broad distinction of the 'three welfare regimes' by Esping-Andersen (1990) and others has a bearing here because each defines the nature of social services differently. The social democratic approach prevalent in the Nordic countries regards the use of social services as a fundamental social right so that the 'merit' of receiving assistance is never at stake. By contrast the residual model of liberalism, particularly in the neo-liberal form, emphasises the need of welfare recipients to prove themselves 'worthy' of the intervention and the representatives of state services always bring a hint of stigma, which professional training can mitigate but not eliminate. Finally, in the corporatist welfare traditions the principle of subsidiarity determines relationships not just between governmental and non-governmental agencies, but also between professionals and volunteers and, above all, representatives of self-help organisations, because the principle always gives priority to informal care and assistance. This stimulates the growth of 'creative' intervention methods geared towards prevention and the preservation or constitution of identity.

Social policy traditions have had a considerable impact on the nature of training in the social professions in Europe. The residual model and the institutional orientation of social policy in the Nordic countries facilitated a strong emphasis on social policy or social administration (as the subject area is sometimes termed in the UK) as a core area of knowledge, especially in social work. Finnish social work curricula have always emphasised research and social policy analysis not just as preliminary academic exercises but as elementary to professional competence, suggesting a framework of practice that constitutes users of social services as citizens with rights, belonging to intricate networks of social solidarity. Unsurprisingly, curricular orientation in the UK tended to be polarised between the fundamentally individualistic case work orientation on the one hand (with subsequent alternative methods still centred on the modification or adaptation of individual behaviour) and the elaboration of community work approaches on the other where the 'political element' became more readily apparent as the critique of the individualism not only of methods but of social service delivery systems spread. In a universalist social policy context, such polarisation featured much less prominently as both methods assumed a complementary function.

Both social policy models also contributed to a more pronounced ranking between the professional profiles of (and hence the status of training for) social work and social education/social care. The social policy structure of services allocates less status (and pay!) to primary carers whose work and methodology gets defined more in procedural terms, where centralised delivery systems leave comparatively little room for creative initiatives and alternatives on the ground. By contrast, the corporatist orientation of welfare traditions, with an emphasis on subsidiarity, stimulated the parallel growth of different, not necessarily hierarchically differentiated, training patterns and professional profiles of various fields of social practice. Apart from the parity of status achieved by social work and social pedagogy in Germany, France also maintained a diversity of fields such as social assistants, special educators and *animateurs* (Jovelin and Tully, 2000). The diversity used to be particularly pronounced in the Netherlands and 'mergers' between some of the professional fields and titles were only a product of the more recent 'streamlining' of Dutch social services and educational structures. This streamlining also swept away the 'pillarisation' of autonomous civil society structures that had safeguarded the diversity of non-governmental social services. However, there are still six distinguishable programmes, leading to qualifications in social work, social pedagogy, creative therapy, community work, social advocacy and personnel and labour management (Freitas, 2004).

In the light of recent profound changes in social policy in all European countries, under the impact of globalisation, this pattern of education in the social professions also began to shift and mutate. The overall effects of these changes can be summarised as occurring at two closely related levels – changes occur in course contents and structures on account of changes in general social policy so that the 'demand side' necessitates adjustments to new practices, structures and principles in social service delivery. They also occur at the level of specific educational policies that alter the 'supply side' of training. Overall, some of the more immediate consequences in terms of course contents are a stronger emphasis on case management in many countries at the expense of the broad range of methods taught previously; a narrowing of the analytical and theoretical orientation of courses, accompanied instead by a stronger emphasis on practice-related outcome and competence; and a general growth of qualifications at post-qualifying level corresponding to demands in the labour market in social services, which tend not to strengthen professional profiles but, on the contrary, dissolve traditional boundaries and identities.

Effects of social policy changes on education and training patterns

To deal with the effects of general social policy changes first, the well-analysed crisis of the welfare state (initially registered in the 1970s) posed a challenge for courses in the social professions throughout Europe. For the historical, professional and sometimes also ideological reasons mentioned above, social work in particular had always sought to maintain a critical distance from the welfare state despite its implicit mandate to contribute to social, political and economic integration; the management of social conflicts; and the stabilisation of capitalism. Nevertheless, training courses in the social professions after the Second World War developed rapidly and confidently against the background of a consensus that welfare services would continue to grow and to consolidate. The stagnation of that expansion, the realisation of the inherent contradictions of the welfare state and finally, the downright ideological critique of its safety-net aspects, caused an acute dilemma for scholars and tutors on training courses. Were they to maintain their critical stance and thereby risk confirming the impression of the professions' inability to service the welfare system on account of their critical sociological bias? Or were they to drop critical reserve, support the more pragmatic implementation of a welfare design that until then had never been given a chance and thereby risk sacrificing professionalism for functionalism? This dilemma caused a general rupture in course orientation everywhere, albeit with considerable modifications mediated by differences in social policy traditions, academic discourses and professional identities in the particular national context. The rupture coincided with the epistemological challenge of post-modernism, which had the effect of injecting methods tutors in particular, but also social policy analysts and to an extent those responsible for teaching psychology subjects, with a tranquillising portion of indifference to the acuteness of the dilemmas posed at the political front. As the 'grand narratives' were being deconstructed, the 'overall picture' began to matter less and less; personal choices were encouraged as legitimate expressions of identity; personal experiences and qualities increased in status in place of scientific analysis and knowledge acquisition; and difference was celebrated, at least for a brief interlude. However, it quickly became apparent that the emancipatory potential of deconstruction, the validation of experience and the differentiation of discrete course elements (modularised and learner-friendly), were easy prey to colonisation by political interests intent on breaking the power of professions and training institutions and on establishing market situations in which the play of supply and demand determined course contents; the relevance of qualifications; and the recruitment of students with suitable backgrounds.

There were significant time lags and modifications in the way those developments manifested themselves in different countries and different professional fields. As the changes occurred at a time when the aforementioned 'indigenisation' of curricula set in, courses and regulatory bodies paid far too little attention to the international character of these trends and failed to reflect on them in terms of cross-national comparisons. Instead, an agenda prevailed in many sectors intent on exploiting the changed framework conditions to consolidate their own particular training tradition or professional profile in the hope of gaining dominance over other fields or at least a higher degree of recognition, without the realisation that market conditions could thereby establish themselves in the training field all the more quickly.

Social policy traditions were a major factor in the differential effects of these changes between countries. Training patterns in countries with an institutional approach to welfare services came under relatively little political pressure and were able to pursue differentiation with a greater degree of autonomy, with competition among fields and approaches creating less adaptation pressures. Courses in Sweden, for instance, gained greater freedom in determining their contents and orientation in the general context of the decentralisation of services there, leading to a higher academic profile of and more explicitly research-based approaches in social work and social pedagogy training (Soydan, 2001). Finland used the opportunity to separate social work training from social policy academic course structures while maintaining a strong research basis, and to implement an inter-university graduate school for social work and social services in their own right (Urponen, 2004). This enables training in those two countries to maintain a critical distance to the practice field while servicing it with relevant research projects and data (Satka and Karvinen, 1999). At the same time AMK (ammattikorkeakoulu) vocational institutions (polytechnics) gained in importance in Finland and now offer degrees in 'social service' (Jacobsson, 1998) with the relationship between university-based courses and non-university tertiary courses being largely uncontroversial.

The Norwegian tradition of three related but separate professions, each with their own training programmes, *sosionom* ('social worker'), *barnevernpedagog* ('child welfare worker') and *vernepleier* ('social educator'), shows little in the way of competition between them. It continues to show little ambition to become more 'academically oriented' and maintains its vocational orientation without therefore becoming more dependent on the immediate training demands from employers, although there are signs that this may be changing (Danbolt and Askeland, 2004). Similarly in Denmark, social work education is located in non-university tertiary institutions with a strong applied orientation but nevertheless offers Masters degrees at two of its five schools (Mason, 2004).

For corporatist welfare regimes, however, the creeping 'marketisation' of social services has triggered a transformation in the meaning and operation of diversity and subsidiarity with subsequent implications for training in the social professions. Superficially, the picture of social professional education in the Netherlands resembles in many ways that of Norway with a plurality of titles and its virtual exclusion from the university sector. Yet here a strengthening trend of independent social service providers bidding for contracts has introduced a considerable element of competition between the professional fields (van der Laan, 1998) and indeed also between schools, which previously had their own stable constituencies of practice agencies that they were servicing. Dutch pragmatism has both adjusted to this market environment and prevented it from obliterating professional responsibility and autonomy.

In Germany, the traditional dualism between social work and social pedagogy, which had always cut across the university–*Fachhochschule* divide, is being superseded by the debate, triggered by social policy changes, on the relevance and value of higher academic qualifications in the light of the erosion of stable ranking patterns in public and semi-public employment. Whereas before, access to senior positions was restricted to holders of university degrees, qualifications that have a strong management bias now begin to assume this importance and *Fachhochschulen* are keen to contest the existing monopoly of universities in conducting research and issuing academic degrees, with all the curricula changes this implies and which the decentralised education system of Germany still permits. So far, the drive by all higher education levels towards gaining or maintaining academic status has been largely inspired by the objective of greater autonomy and distance from employer pressure, but this supply-side orientation is subtly shifting towards demand-led criteria of curriculum design.

The convergence on a social management concept has also characterised developments in Austria where the category of 'Akademie' as a particular non-university, professional training institution for social work was recently abolished to be replaced, not by university degree courses, but by new *Fachhochschulen*, which operate as private trusts or limited companies and have a strong leaning towards case management, especially where they are also offering courses in management and business administration. By contrast, the transition from 'higher schools' to Fachhochschulen in Switzerland shows no such bias and has produced highly vibrant, research-promoting and professional quality-oriented courses.

In France, the pronounced divide between the university and the non-university sector of third-level education, to which all sectors of the social professions were later almost exclusively relegated, weakened the professions' autonomy in the face of the government's relentless drive towards decentralisation and private–public partnerships in social services. Here diversity manifested itself in a highly liberalised market of largely unregulated qualifications, some of them now university based, with a strong emphasis on techno-managerial skills. 'These changes have occurred within both the third sector and in statutory public services, which are increasingly adopting a positivist, empirically justified, cost-efficiency culture' (Jovelin and Tully, 2000, p. 46).

The most acute tensions within any of the European training traditions in the social professions occurred in the UK and this, like the unparalleled onslaught on social workers in general on the part of Conservative politicians and sections of the media (on the occasion of reports on incidents of poor practice), can be directly attributed to the residualism as the key construct of British social policy. In no other social policy tradition does social work carry such a strong symbolic function, alongside its pragmatic usefulness, in marking and policing a fundamental frontier in society between the public and the private domain, between self-reliance and dependence, between the deserving and the undeserving. Social work in particular had managed to build up a respectable and respected degree of autonomy and professionalism within this basic structure through the well-balanced nature of its training patterns between academic and vocational orientation, but it was unable to safeguard these achievements once politics radically changed the coordinates that mapped the meaning of those divides. The race to regain, if not autonomy, at least a breathing space by remodelling the strong, scientifically grounded methods epistemology of the Anglo-Saxon training tradition into a competence-led pattern of discrete outcomes could not be won because social policy targets in the practice field kept changing and foresaw no consolidation of those competences into integrated professional profiles. On the contrary, those targets favoured further fragmentation and concentrated on functional analyses and performance indicators (Adams and Shardlow, 2000), thereby not permitting any real purchase on practice and agency developments on the part of the academic field by means of either fundamental analytical critique or of constructive conformity.

The most obvious effects of social policies on training in the social professions, however, can be observed in the countries of CEE. Developments after 1989 can serve as a live laboratory for studying the dynamics that unfold between state policies, educational interests, civil society initiatives and movements and market forces (Constable and Mehta, 1994). To many western observers from government departments, and educational and welfare institutions, the situation after the end of Communism presented the opportunity to move in and 'start from zero' because officially social work and hence training in social work had not existed in the countries of the Soviet block. This perception totally ignored and did injustice to both the memories of pre-communist beginnings of training and practice; and to the determined efforts on the part of some individuals and institutions to keep those traditions alive or to launch new initiatives under very difficult political circumstances. Programmes at professionalising practice through systematic training had existed in Czechoslovakia, Estonia, Hungary and Poland since the 1920s and 1930s. In Poland Helena Radlinska founded a school within the Free University of Warsaw in 1925 based on principles of social pedagogy and students of hers contributed to the founding of further schools in the 1960s (Marynowicz-Hetka, 1999). Hungary, in the early parts of the 20th century, had followed the tradition of 'settlements', neighbourhood centres of social assistance and social transformation, which developed their own social policy research base. Sociologists in collaboration with Szusza Ferge at Budapest University built on this tradition, which had continued after 1948 to prepare a social science-based training programme for social work even before this became formally possible in 1990 (Pik, 1999). In former Yugoslavia five higher schools of social work were founded between 1953 and 1960 of which three were integrated into university faculties in 1985 (Pešič and Jovanovič, 1986).

The changes after 1989 gave new impetus to training initiatives from inside and outside former Communist countries. On the one hand, there was an urgent need to train a whole stratum of professionals who had a vital role to play in stabilising societies thrown into turmoil by the sudden disappearance of basic income securities. On the other hand, trainers within those countries needed to ward off the rush of offers to 'help' and establish course models to Western patterns in order to create some space for autonomous, 'indigenous' models to grow. In the end a broad range of training models and professional directions became established, which resemble Western European patterns but which have, by now, been subjected to a great deal of critical, autonomous scrutiny and adjusted to local and regional conditions. Training is located at both the university and the non-university level of tertiary education, both the social work and the social pedagogy traditions are represented there and systems adapt relatively easily to the demands of the Bologna Declaration.

Implications of the Bologna Process

In all parts of Europe these social policy changes and their impact on courses in the social professions in Europe intersect with and are compounded by the so-called Bologna Process. In a declaration issued at the Sorbonne University in France in 1998, which took the academic world by surprise and which did not connect organically with the experiences gained through the steady growth of international contacts and cooperation that the EU programmes had facilitated, ministers of culture and education from France, Germany, Italy and the UK expressed their intention of harmonising higher education qualifications according to a three-stage model of awards – Bachelor, Master and Ph.D. This was followed by the Bologna Declaration in 1999 in which 29 European ministers laid the foundation for the creation of a 'European Higher Education Area', which facilitated mobility through uniform credit, quality and recognition systems centred on the '3 + 2' principle (a three-year undergraduate degree followed by two-year post-graduate degrees), which was to be discussed in all countries, with reference to the English titles of Bachelor and Master. This was without any reference to other educational histories and the cultural divergence of existing titles in the European languages, and can be viewed as an act of incomprehensible cultural insensitivity. For the social professions this process, which is continuing in ever-expanding circles of participating countries, poses a dual challenge (Seibel, 2004). On the one hand, they are forced to adjust the varying lengths of qualifying courses to the new numeric pattern; on the other hand, it creates the necessity to translate existing systems governing the relationship between academic and professional course elements into a new, standardised, quantitatively defined system of credits and quality criteria.

For a professional field that is so widely distributed over the various forms of third-level education and that so far had only had the opportunity of negotiating the meaning of the relationship between these educational characteristics and their correspondence in the practice and employment field (locally or nationally), these changes are bound to set off a fundamental dichotomy. They partly become the vehicle for the 'up-grading' of qualifications where the path to equivalence with higher levels had seemed barred on account of national conventions and traditions, but they also contain the danger of reducing the professional element of training, by subjecting it to purely academic quality criteria, and, what is more, academic criteria that are largely not defined from within an 'indigenous' discipline. The mere distinction of the two degrees alludes to a hierarchical distinction in which the Master level is bound to be regarded as 'higher' and hence 'better' whereas in fact the criteria that would endorse and legitimate this distinction are rendered more abstract and formal than had been the case in the hard-won agreements over existing qualifying levels and qualification titles. Since the majority of European social work courses so far were of more than three years' duration to qualifying level, the debate over the new '3 + 2' standard resembles the reactions to a Gestalt test picture. Some see in it the chance of upgrading the qualification to an overall five-year package of high academic prestige; others regard it as a downgrading since the threshold itself will mean a de facto exit point for a majority of students who will be absorbed in some way or other by the employment market. The Master level will cater for an elite who, in all likelihood, will be entering managerial or specialised positions where the 'added value' of their qualification only benefits the mainstream of services indirectly.

Accordingly, the adoption of the Bologna criteria proves to be quite uncontentious in some countries, whereas in others it has given rise to ardent debate and controversy. Indeed, the former Communist countries of CEE adjust most easily to the patterns as they offer a relatively economical but status-oriented solution that helps to establish the social position of these professions unambiguously. Social work courses in the UK generally regard themselves as winners in the process having finally abolished the European anomaly of a less than three-year qualifying standard. However, there are also immediate losses in terms of the reduction in the number of Master programmes and conversion courses leading to the qualifying level, which had been a valuable supplement to the overall professional profile of social work. It remains to be seen how long the existing four-year Bachelor courses, a central plank of professional training in the case of the Republic of Ireland, will continue under the Bologna pressure and whether the old demand, put forward by the Irish Association of Social Workers, for a five-year qualifying level, will prevail.

Courses in social work in Italy are also indirect winners from the process which prompted little debate in the universities. Social work had risked being at a disadvantage in relation to social pedagogy, in as much as courses in the latter discipline originally adopted the 'proper' university standard for first degrees (*Laurea*) of four years, being as it were, an offspring of general pedagogy courses at universities. Social work courses, on account of their history in the non-university sector (see above), were given only the status of a '*Laurea breve*' of three years, but the Bologna Process begins to level the difference with the general '3 + 2' pattern. Ironically, the 'two extra' (pi~ due) are giving rise to numerous misunderstandings because thus far the title 'Master' had very little status in Italian universities, being a qualification that had only a minimal disciplinary base and could be awarded for highly specific training courses (for example, family therapy), whereas the academic *più due* was called '*Laurea specialistica*'. This terminology is about to change but against the objection that the title 'Master' has no academic appeal; and that the change from 'old' to 'new' Master courses will mean (once more) a loss of the professional element since these academic courses are minutely prescribed by ministerial regulations, which are in turn dictated by the power blocks of established university disciplines.

The most ardent debate on the Bologna Process rages in Germany where proponents and opponents of the Bachelor/Master model, as it is termed there, are equally fixated on the length of training by which quality standards become implicitly defined, instead of allowing a measured debate on expectations, contents and standards first. Old enmities erupt anew, between *Fachhochschulen* and universities and between social work and social pedagogy.

If the pattern were to be introduced, as seems likely at the time of writing (2004), equally at both institutional levels and in both disciplines, universities would lose out on two counts; first, through the shortening of the basic qualification (which, as a university diploma, was previously of four to five years' duration) and second, through the loss of the dominant position in higher qualifications and the concomitant research emphasis (Otto, 2004). Market forces, in line with government economy drives, will favour shortening and diversification, leaving the quality standard question wide open. Accreditation of course programmes in Germany has moved from the Länder ministries to an uncoordinated plethora of accreditation enterprises with very little tie-in with the professions themselves, which have always been poorly organised in Germany. Already the uncoordinated growth of Master programmes there is indicative: Pfaffenberger, himself a pioneer of German post-war social work education, in a critical overview lambastes the exoticism of titles like 'Master of Non-Profit-Administration', 'Master of Consulting' and 'Master of Art in Sex Education and Family Planning' (Pfaffenberger, 2004, p. 68).

Conclusion

A political analysis of these changes in Germany gives an indication of the 'backstage developments' that exert their pressure on higher education generally and on training in social (and educational) professions in particular. As Elsen (2004) and Wallimann (2004) point out, the drive for the implementation of compatibility between countries and institutions stems from the General Agreement on Trade in Services (GATS) framework of the World Trade Organisation to which all European countries have signed up and which seeks to exploit the commercial potential of education and social services by reducing regulatory barriers and fiscal inconsistencies. European harmonisation of training patterns, seen in this light, paves the way for deregulation and gives a further indication that developments in education for the social professions can only be understood from a perspective that pays attention to fundamental changes in social and educational policies simultaneously.

As always in the history of the social professions, current trends in training point in different directions simultaneously. Formally, the course formats are being driven towards greater uniformity and are being subjected to greater scrutiny as the entire Bologna Process is accompanied by new academic quality control measures. As far as contents and professional orientation are concerned, they are headed for greater discrepancies and a demand-led, increasingly marketised differentiation. The rise of the social management paradigm is symptomatic of this ambiguity, as it offers a black box construct of compatibility and universality, which brackets out fundamental critical discourses on epistemology, political values and ethics. It remains to be seen whether intensifying cross-national analytical comparisons can help the professional fields to regain a degree of initiative and autonomy in the interest of the development of quality criteria, which are accountable to the users of social services.

Chapter 4

Research and Professional Education

Karen Lyons

Introduction

As previous chapters have indicated, there have been significant changes in national and European climates, which have affected the landscape of professional education for the social welfare sector. This chapter suggests that these changes have also impacted on the amount and characteristics of research taking place in the social professional field as much as other areas of education, policy and practice. It can be argued that research is a necessary part of professional development at the individual level; of disciplinary development (in relation to education and training opportunities); and of the development of policies, practices and services that are based on a better understanding of emerging and entrenched social concerns and possible responses to them. Indeed, within an educational context, research is sometimes seen as the third point of a triangle whose other points include education (or theory) and practice, between which there is a dynamic and interactive relationship (Powell, 2002; Lovelock et al., 2004).

This chapter examines whether research is seen as a necessary part of professional education in Europe; the opportunities and limitations with regard to its inclusion in the curriculum; and the variation in approaches favoured in different European countries. It also considers the extent to which research is being carried out from a comparative perspective (that is, comparing and contrasting policy and/or practice situations across two or more countries). But first, attention is given to the macro-context within which research is carried out at national and European levels through some consideration of the social policies and institutional frameworks that are shaping demands and opportunities for research.

The macro-context: Changing policies and opportunities

As suggested in Part 1, there has been a significant shift in thinking about welfare systems and provisions over (approximately) the past two decades across the EU15 and European Free Trade Association countries and, since about 1990, in the case of Central and Eastern Europe (CEE) states. Changes in political ideology and practical funding arrangements associated with the marketisation of welfare have had an impact on the roles and expectations of social professionals, and therefore on education and training programmes.

A major factor in the changes has been an increase in concern about value for money (efficiency and effectiveness) resulting not only in increased managerialism and regulation but also in greater attention to monitoring and evaluation. To some extent this has driven both the formulation of research agendas and the establishment of new research agencies. In some cases it has also affected the expectations about the type of research approach favoured by national governments, with stated concerns that research should lead to 'evidence-based practice' evident in the Nordic countries and the UK (Gould, 2004). This emphasis is perhaps less apparent in the policies of the European Union (EU) and other bi-lateral or supranational funding bodies, which often have a stated concern for transnational knowledge transfer. The extent to which the higher education sector and social professional organisations contribute to new initiatives or are seen as reacting to them is variable. Some examples of recent and current research arrangements and developments at national and European levels are now presented to illustrate these points.

The case of Finland

Finland is part of the Nordic region and enjoys the benefits of the Nordic welfare state model and a high standard of living. However, it also shares social concerns common to other advanced industrial countries, including the effects of globalisation on the domestic economy; an increase in the diversification and privatisation of social welfare provision; and demographic change. In relation to demographic change, for instance, the proportion of people over 65 years of age is set to nearly double from 15% in 2000 to 26% by 2030 (Juntunen and Hämäläinen, 2001). In these circumstances there are demands on social professionals to participate in social planning as well as service delivery in both traditional and newer areas of practice. An example of the latter would be the relatively recent establishment of minority ethnic populations (related to the arrival of asylum seekers in the 1990s) who are more likely to experience economic need and social marginalisation (see, for instance, Okitikpi and Aymer, 2000).

In terms of the participation of social work education and research at the European level, Finland may be said to have emerged fairly recently, following a relatively late establishment of social work from the 1940s and a period of introversion and concern with locating itself nationally. Karvinen et al. (1999) have suggested that Finland had a strong and explicit research base in the 1980s but that (female) 'experience-based knowledge' was displaced by efforts to strengthen the status of social work through the introduction of positivist social research methods (which at the same time also increased the gap between theory and practice). In the 1990s, social work-trained lecturers regained control of the research programmes, which has resulted in the (re-) establishment of more practice-orientated research and more emphasis on research methods that are congruent with and part of a repertoire of reflective skills.

From an outsider perspective, social work education and research now seem to be well established in the university sector, relative to some other countries, and to be working positively with social welfare agencies, locally and nationally. A concrete example of the extent to which knowledge creation and development of professional practice is seen as a shared enterprise – and one supported by the state – has been evidenced in the recent establishment of nine 'Competence Centres' where education, research and practice are undertaken collaboratively. While the structure echoes a model more commonly found in the medical field, the initiators and staff espouse the development of research methodologies appropriate to the analysis of social and relationship problems and relevant interventions (Karvinen, 2003a).

Notable also among the institutional arrangements for research in the social professional field is the existence of a body called SOSNET, which comprises a national network of all those universities involved in social work education (six, including one in Lapland). This body provides joint training for a professional licentiate and for doctoral studies at a national level, as well as cooperating on issues related to undergraduate studies, in a teaching project, and in international developments. Unlike most countries in Europe, Finland has already established a national database of doctoral degrees, including social work, of which the recent/current output is about 25 per annum (Karvinen, 2003b).

Recent research developments in the UK

Meanwhile, in a larger and more diverse society, the modernisation agenda of the UK around the turn of the 21st century has had a significant impact on the social work and social care scene, not least related to the restructuring of how social work services are delivered and the regulatory frameworks for practice, service provision and education. In this situation there are two particular ways in which changes are impacting on the research environment: one related to the field of practice and the other related more generally to the higher education setting of professional education.

A major development in the field of practice has been the establishment (since 2001) of a specific agency (funded by, but independent of, the government), the Social Care Institute for Excellence (commonly known as SCIE). The remit of this organisation is to foster research and, more particularly, to ensure that the findings of research are translated into useable knowledge for the practitioners and managers of social work. A major aim is to develop knowledge for practice not only from the findings of conventional research projects but also from research and evaluation studies in which service users are participants (rather than the 'subjects' of research). An early exercise by one review team was to undertake a 'knowledge review' about the types and quality of knowledge in social care. This produced a discussion document that suggested a classification of knowledge type according to its source (a service user or carer, a social worker, or a researcher), stating that different types of knowledge deserve equal respect and attention. However, the team acknowledged that there must be a quality assessment of the knowledge produced from different sources and proposed a framework using the concepts of transparency; accuracy; purposivity; utility; propriety; accessibility; and specificity as criteria (SCIE, 2003).

In addition to SCIE, there is a range of professional associations, including a Social Services Research Group (SSRG) and a Social Work Research Association (SWRA), which provide opportunities for networking and other activities by those social professionals directly involved in the production or use of research. Social work educators may also belong to the British Association of Social Workers (BASW) (whose Code of Ethics 2001 includes a reference to ethical conduct in relation to research), and most are represented in the Joint University Council Social Work Education Committee (JUC SWEC). The latter has given considerable attention to promoting the research profile of the discipline (particularly in the period since 1999), alongside the pressing concerns of restructuring social work education into primarily a three-year undergraduate programme (from 2003 in England, where some opportunities continue for students with other first degrees to gain a professional qualification at post-graduate level, and from 2004 in Northern Ireland, Scotland and Wales).

More generally, in the context of higher education, a periodic, UK-wide Research Assessment Exercise (RAE) invites submissions from any subject in any university as a way of assessing quality and awarding research funding. This exercise (most recently carried out in 2001 and due to take place again in 2008) has attracted an increasing number of submissions from social work to a specialist panel. The 2001 RAE provided a 'snapshot' of the sort of research being carried out in the discipline and over time also provides an indication of relative trends, for instance with regard to subject matter, methodology and levels of staff participation. Shaw (2003), drawing on an Overview Report, suggested that the 2001 exercise demonstrated increased theoretical literacy in social work research, while also illuminating the processes and outcomes of practice, and providing evidence of greater attention to user involvement.

Therefore, in the UK, despite a relatively recent history in which research did not have a high profile in professional education, there is currently a climate that can be said to be favourable to the development of social work research in various forms, and previous deficiencies are being addressed in the period 2003-06 through targeted funding aimed at enhancing the research capacity of the subject. Social professionals can also apply for funding of (usually collaborative) projects from a range of sources, including from governmental bodies (for example, the Department of Health, the Department for Education and Skills or the Economic and Social Research Council) and from long-established charitable foundations (such as the Joseph Rowntree Charitable Trust). Additionally, some social professionals carry out small-scale research projects (often without funding) as practitioner-researchers or academics, sometimes as part of post-professional studies or doctoral research programmes (see later and also Chapter 7). Further, while UK staff did not necessarily coordinate bids for European or international projects, there has been some participation in EU-funded networks (often over a decade or more). These have had research 'spin-offs' or have had research as a primary goal.

Promoting research in CEE countries

The examples of Finland and the UK represent countries where research has become an established aspect of social work education and of professional activity more broadly. Regulatory mechanisms, including professional codes of conduct and registration requirements are in place and, relatively speaking, there is encouragement and funding for research activities. This can be contrasted with the situation in some of the CEE accession countries. For instance, although social work education has been developed in Lithuania since 1991 and is now offered by 10 universities, the Lithuanian Association of Social Work Schools is still in its infancy and there are much greater concerns about resources and research capacity – a situation that is mirrored in countries such as Poland and the Ukraine, as well as Russia (personal communications). However, interestingly, in the Czech Republic a Society for Social Workers was established in 1990, followed three years later by an Association of Educators in Social Work. A code of Ethics was agreed in 1995 and programmes are available at undergraduate, postgraduate and doctoral levels in four universities (Chytil, 2002).

In this situation the availability of funding from outside a country has particular attractions, even if offered only in the context of collaborative activities with partners from other countries (which can be seen as a constraint as well as an opportunity!), and the EU and other funding bodies have been important in providing and developing resources.

An example of the utilisation of EU funding to develop research resources was evident in a Tempus programme aimed at promoting social work education at Mohyla Academy, Kiev (Ukraine) in which a tutor from Anglia Polytechnic University (UK) delivered an intensive one-week programme about social research methods to social workers at the Academy (over successive years in the late 1990s), laying the basis for mainstreaming research teaching by local staff for all students. In Lithuania, more recently, a three-week summer school (funded by the Open Society Institute in 2001 and 2002 and held at Vytautas Magnus University, Kaunas) was attended by over 20 educators (each year) from a range of CEE states (nine in 2002). Students were offered teaching by American and British educators and the programme included time for guidance about small-scale projects that participants would carry out following the course. These were usually about service developments in particular sectors or localities and, apart from testing out students' new learning and developing teaching material, projects could also be useful in contributing to the research and knowledge base about developing responses to social problems in CEE countries.

The EU and research initiatives

Alongside its action programme to create a European Higher Education Area (EHEA) (discussed in Chapter 2), the EU aims to create a European Research Area (ERA) by 2010. Together the EHEA and ERA are seen as the two pillars necessary to promote a 'Europe of Knowledge' (Berlin Communiqué, 2003). Research had already been explicitly mentioned in three of the five principles articulated in the 1998 Magna Charta for European Universities. The universities themselves are seen as having a primary role in the promotion of universal and intercultural knowledge, and also as being concerned with transmission of culture and the maintenance of a European humanist tradition. Research is seen as one means (the other being teaching) through which these goals are achieved; and is identified as being inseparable from teaching; and an area where academic freedom should operate.

However, research was not a significant focus of the Bologna Declaration and there was some concern about where research fits in to the two-cycle (Bachelor /Master) structure and how Master- and doctoral-level teaching are related (Corbett, 2003). To some extent the latter point was subsequently addressed in the Berlin Communiqué (2003), which formally identified doctoral work as the third cycle in higher education and noted the importance of research and research training (together with the promotion of interdisciplinarity and inter-institutional activities) in improving European higher education. Ministers also pledged support (including financial) for the development of doctoral student mobility and networks; and for improved access to data banks and research results. One initiative has already been taken in the social professional field in relation to increasing participation of doctoral students in European activities with the holding of an International Summer School in St Petersburg in 2003 and 2004 (www.mapping-the-way-forward.net/news.html).

Together with new members agreed in Berlin, the EHEA extends beyond current EU membership and by early 2004 included 40 countries. However, despite formal membership of EHEA and implied acceptance of the Magna

Charta and the Bologna Declaration, it seems likely that individual countries are differently influenced by European declarations. For instance, it is possible that current trends in UK policy may separate research from teaching (due to a preference for funding research in specialist Centres of Excellence), thereby contravening one of the principles of the Magna Charta Universitatum (www.magna-charta.org/home.html); and the extent to which 'academic freedom' is a reality or constrained by regulatory and funding mechanisms is also variable. However, the overall European climate has recently favoured the development of cross-national networks that have research and knowledge creation as a primary focus (rather than, for instance, student mobility) and social professionals have been able to bid for funding alongside other disciplines.

Specifically, the Fifth Framework (funding) programme included 'Accompanying Measures for Improving the Human Research Potential for the Socio-economic Knowledge Base Programme', the fourth measure of which aimed to create new knowledge and to find ways to access this knowledge (Laot, 2004). One beneficiary of this programme was the CERTS Project (*Centre Europeén de Ressources pour la Recherche en Travail Social*/European Resource Centre for Social Work Research, 2002–04 (www.certs-europe.com). This network, led by a French School (*Ecole Superieure de Travail Social* or ETSUP, in Paris), and initially including schools in 10 countries (but subsequently extended) focused on the establishment of a European-wide database of doctoral theses and other significant research projects in the field of social work. 'Social work' was broadly defined to recognise national differences in occupational titles and boundaries, and the database aimed to raise the visibility and accessibility of relevant research output as well as providing a source of information about the focus and methodology of research activities in the social professional field. (It can be noted in passing that Dellgran and Hojer (2003) have undertaken an analysis of topics and methodologies of doctoral theses in Sweden, but there do not appear to have been similar national studies elsewhere as yet).

One area not addressed much in this chapter concerns interdisciplinary or interprofessional research. However, at the time of writing it seems that both the EU and some national funding bodies are increasingly favouring funding applications that represent different 'stakeholders' (including user groups) or research teams that cut across disciplinary and professional boundaries. Such an emphasis reflects the recognition of the multifaceted nature of many social problems and the value of bringing different perspectives to bear on their analysis. It seems likely that, to date, such teams have rarely included social professionals (although this may be more likely in some national contexts than others), and there is clearly scope for development.

Even without the new emphasis being given to interdisciplinarity, it has been suggested that teaching social research discretely to students and/or seeking to establish the distinctive nature of social work research could isolate social professions from the wider scientific community (Thyer, 2000, speaking from an American perspective) and/or from the range of other professional groups (for example, health care staff, teachers, town planners) who are also concerned about the impact of particular problems on their field of work. However, it can be argued that there may be good reasons to focus particularly on research developments within the discipline and profession at this time in Europe. Such reasons include the need to build research capacity and confidence (in some countries) and also to progress developments in particular approaches and methodologies that seem most congruent with the goals and values of social professionals (in many countries). Again, there are indications that social professionals might benefit from recent initiatives at European level, as the European Science Foundation announced (in 2004) a project to look at the development of qualitative methods in the social sciences. This seems an appropriate point to turn to further consideration of approaches and methods being taught to students and used in research by social professionals.

Education and training for social professionals: Research and the curriculum

In most European countries, higher expectations are being placed on social professionals in terms of analytical skills in order to better understand the complex and dynamic interplay of interpersonal and societal (including cross-national) forces impacting on individual behaviour and the situation of selected groups or whole communities. Professionals are expected to be able to identify trends, anticipate areas of difficulty and devise imaginative programmes to address a wide range of social problems. This suggests that teaching about research should be a requirement of all forms of professional education. From the wording of a questionnaire circulated globally in 1999–2000 (Lyons, 2000), it was clearly an assumption of the International Association of Schools of Social Work (IASSW) that research would be included in the curriculum; and a recent document Global Qualifying Standards for Social Work Education and Training (IASSW, 2005) also suggests that teaching about research should be an integral part of professional education.

However, what does 'teaching about research' mean, and what are the factors that affect the extent to which research (in some form) is likely to be included in curricula? It can be argued that there is a close association between the likelihood that research will be included in the curriculum (and be a recognised part of the educators' role) and the level at which social professional education is provided, as well as the duration of courses.

While virtually all forms of education for social professionals are provided within the tertiary sector, not all schools or courses preparing students for social work and allied practice are located within the university sector. This affects the extent to which educators themselves are expected to be research active, as well as whether institutions can award a first or higher degree. Thus, in countries reflecting different welfare and educational arrangements, students may not be awarded a degree even for up to four years of study at higher education level; and the institutions awarding professional qualifications (for instance, Technical Education Institutes in Greece or *Hogeschoolen* in the Netherlands) cannot offer research degrees. However, this is not to say that research methods will not be taught – they are a recognised part of both Greek and Dutch qualifying courses (personal communications). It can be suggested, therefore, that the inclusion or not of research teaching in the curriculum might be more related to the length of the course than its presumed academic level.

The British situation provides an illustration of this point, since for some time (up to 2003) research methods teaching was not a required or integral part of up to 50% of qualifying courses that were carried out over two years, resulting in a Diploma in Higher Education (with a relevant professional diploma) rather than a degree (Lyons, 1999b). There was, however, increasingly an expectation that social professionals would be 'research informed', through the use of examples of research in the teaching of all units or modules. Students could thus be expected to demonstrate both an understanding of some of the major theories arising from significant research carried out in the contributory disciplines (psychology and the social sciences); and also knowledge of the most recent findings in key areas of welfare policy and professional practice. Associated concepts were 'research awareness' and 'research mindedness', conveying the expectation that newly qualified social workers would be aware that research on a given topic might be available and that they would be able to access and utilise relevant findings.

There were insufficient responses from the European region to the previously mentioned IASSW survey to give reliable data about the teaching of research methods in social professional courses. However, it seems likely that most students across Europe do have exposure to social research as an area of knowledge and practice and that formal teaching about 'research methods' is an identifiable aspect of the curriculum in many courses at undergraduate and postgraduate level (whether qualifications are formally awarded from within the university sector or not). But, this perception is challenged where there has been an emphasis on competency for practice, as for instance, in the case of Danish social work education, where there is no reserved place for teaching about research in new curriculum developments (personal communication).

Other questions then arise, for instance about the stage at which research methods are taught; the depth/range of knowledge about research methods that students might be expected to learn; whether courses (units or modules) are geared to the needs and interests of social professionals in particular or taught by a social researcher to a wider range of social science and/or professional students; and whether the students have the opportunity to carry out some empirical work through a small-scale individual or group project. Unfortunately there has not yet been systematic comparative research about the curricula of social professional courses to give definitive answers to these questions. However, it is possible to make some observations at a general level about the stage of teaching, methodologies, and project work based on the experience of the author and others.

The stage at which research methods might or should be taught

There is sometimes an assumption that research is an 'advanced' area of knowledge to be introduced in the final year of undergraduate courses, or sometimes even delayed as being primarily the province of Master- and doctoral-level work. However, Lorenz (2003) has made a powerful case for including teaching about research from the first year of undergraduate courses and suggests that, if coupled with practical tasks, this can make an important contribution to how students learn about social work. Citing his experience in first-year research teaching at the Free University of Bolzano (Italy), he suggests that the method adopted introduces students to the importance of not only 'what we know' but 'how we know' and that recognition of the validity of different ways of knowing parallels ideas about different ways of intervening.

On a more technical level, some courses, for instance in the UK, place emphasis in first-year teaching on the development of information literacy skills, so that students are confident about the use of web-based resources. These often provide useful contextual information or even raw data (for example, through newspaper articles) from which to develop research questions and begin investigating specific social phenomena. Such units may then form the basis for an approach to teaching and (experiential) learning about research that constitutes an element (or pillar) at each stage of the professional course, in which classroom teaching and exercises are complemented by opportunities for empirical work through individual or group projects (see later).

But clearly there is sometimes scope for social professionals to learn (more) about social research in post-qualifying and continuing professional development programmes (see Chapter 7) or through carrying out their own programme of research for a higher degree. With regard to research degrees, there is variation across Europe between countries where it is possible for social professionals to register for a Master of Philosophy or doctoral degree in a social work (or similarly named) school or department − or where they can only register under the auspices of a discipline such as psychology or sociology. Drawing on information from presentations at a CERTS Project Seminar in 2002, there are generally more opportunities to undertake 'social work' doctoral research or even 'professional doctorates' (in the UK) in Northern European countries relative to the likelihood that people in France and Southern Europe will undertake doctoral research under the supervision of a range of other disciplines (see also Laot, 2000). It is more difficult to generalise about CEE countries, but a number are making serious efforts to establish their own doctoral programmes (for example, as in Lithuania and the Czech Republic) or, in some cases, are enabling educators (in particular) to register at universities of Western Europe (or the US) to pursue research (for example, Estonia).

So far the development of 'professional doctorates' (usually undertaken part time by social professionals working 'in the field') or achieving a doctoral degree through publication (normally only open to people already engaged in academic work) seems to be limited to the UK and some Nordic countries rather than being forms that are widely available to social professionals throughout Europe (Lyons, 2002, 2003). However doctoral programmes are structured, the possibility of social professionals contributing to the knowledge base of social work and social care 'from the inside' is potentially important for addressing social problems (in the European context as well as at national levels) and may also encourage subsequent participation in interdisciplinary research.

Research paradigms (or approaches) and methodology

The brief mention of opportunities for doctoral work also relates to the wider question of the research paradigms and data collection methods that may be identified as relevant to social professionals and thus included in their education and training programmes. The tensions between 'academic respectability' (assumed to be attained through positivistic and predominantly quantitative research) and congruence with professional methods and values (thought to be more likely in interpretive and qualitative approaches), mentioned in the previously described Finnish case, is to some extent replicated in other Northern European countries and reflected in the syllabus of specific research units. However, more broadly, it is possible to identify again, significant differences in emphases in research methods teaching between countries in Northern and Southern Europe, which do not necessarily seem to be related to public or governmental expectations of research, nor to the type of institution within which social work is taught, nor to the length of courses.

Thus, in general, interpretive approaches with a focus on a research question (rather than hypothesis) seem to be favoured in some Northern European countries, while there are indications that more traditional conceptions of research (as comprising quantitative studies, perhaps setting out to prove or disprove a hypothesis) are the favoured approaches in Southern European countries. Evidence for this assertion comes from various quarters. These include the research design and methodologies of projects undertaken by students of different nationalities on postgraduate courses (such as the MA in Comparative European Social Studies (Reverda and Richardson, 2000) or the MA in International Social Work – see Chapter 7) and the findings from the earlier-mentioned project examining doctoral work in Europe (Laot, 2000).

With regard to possible reasons for national differences, Lorenz (2003) has described the origins of social research as being in a positivist epistemology in the Anglo-American tradition (from which some British social work educators have sought to develop alternative approaches) and reflecting a more hermeneutic tradition in (some) continental European countries. However, it can also be suggested that these differences are related to the extent to which social professional education is carried out in institutions where the status and values of 'traditional disciplines' (rather than professional education) prevail and that there is also a gender dimension in the differences (Lyons and Taylor, 2004).

Meanwhile, countries in CEE are trying to identify what will be the most useful research paradigms to them in the wider context of striving to establish the place of social professionals, and the educational courses on which they are trained, in the new social order. Approaches to research teaching are likely to be affected by two factors. The first is that many people who are now social work educators have come from different disciplinary and professional backgrounds (such as psychology, teaching or medicine), bringing with them knowledge and assumptions about particular ways of designing and carrying out research projects from previous experience. The second is related to the possibility that initially staff development for those who become social work educators will come from another country (often in Western Europe), so that dominant paradigms or favoured methodologies will be 'imported' from elsewhere. This was to some extent evident in the focus on practitioner research and evaluative studies in the Lithuanian Summer School mentioned earlier (although it could also be argued that there was prior knowledge and negotiation about the orientation of external contributors).

Turning to other specific examples, Shaw (2003) noted that some of the submissions to the UK RAE evidenced particular strengths in qualitative research but that there was a paucity of quantitative research, and he suggested that much could be learned from the traditions of evaluative research developed in the US. Similarly, he advocated for greater collaboration in research across professional boundaries (for example, between social work and health or education). In relation to collaborative research, it can be noted that there has been some emphasis on the development of practitioner research in both health and education (which provides some useful models for social professional research); and it can also be observed that there has been some development of the action-research approach, mainly in the educational context (Hart and Bond, 1995).

Both these approaches resonate in some other European countries. For instance, the book by Karvinen et al. (1999) contains a number of examples of practitioner research in the Finnish context, and the concept is also familiar to Swedish and Danish social professionals. It is possible (but not inevitable) that some practitioner research may demonstrate a form of action research (that is concerned with effecting change in a situation through the research process, rather than, perhaps, only evaluating change). Lorenz (2003) has noted the relative lack of popularity of this approach (following its significant use in the US and UK in the 1960s and later in Germany). This could be attributed to the ambivalence about researchers becoming 'change agents' and thus part of a process in which power and knowledge are shared (at least in part) with non-researchers. This can be contrasted with the traditional view of the researcher as an objective expert, external to the situation being researched. However, the issue of power sharing comes up in another approach currently being advocated by some, for example in the UK, namely, participative research, in which particular service users or community groups, for instance, are enabled to contribute to setting the research agenda, designing a project and participating in all the stages of the research process (Reason and Bradbury, 2001).

Similarly the question of 'insider status' is one faced by many practitioner-researchers, and, more generally, is at the heart of the question about whether social professionals can research their own field of practice. This has been conceptualised as 'nearness to' or 'distance from' the research subject by a Danish social work educator (Rasmussen, 2000). It is also possible to link this concern to the challenge in the British social research literature to traditional social research theory and practice posed by feminist researchers and again this is a perspective that is accepted as being relevant and important in some UK teaching about social work research (theory and practice) (Humphries, 1999, 2004).

However, the earlier-mentioned political goal of ensuring value for money of publicly provided or funded services, is likely to favour 'hard data' of the sort that positivistic research designs and quantitative methods are expected to produce. It can therefore be argued that there is a need for teaching about (and application of) both approaches and 'mixed methodology', rather than assuming that a 'one size fits all' approach is any more appropriate in research than it would be in policy or practice. This view is being reflected in the UK in higher expectations about the range of research methods that social professionals will be taught, particularly at postgraduate level, if they wish to benefit from research student funding opportunities available through the Economic and Social Research Council (ESRC). There are also advocates for higher expectations of undergraduates with regard to numeracy and appreciation (if not application) of quantitative research methods.

The foregoing represents a tangential consideration of the way in which values are likely to impact on social research. It is generally agreed in the (UK) social research literature that all researchers come from a particular standpoint and that this affects both their choice of topic and their approach, that is, the idea that (social) research is value free has been refuted (May, 2001). However, this is also an appropriate point at which to examine another issue important in the teaching and conduct of social research, namely ethical considerations. In some European countries there has been an increase in attempts to regulate the conduct of occupational groups, including researchers, through the specification of ethical codes and, in the case of research, the establishment of bodies concerned to give ethical approval to proposed projects. Nationally, it is also increasingly likely that data gathered in the course of research will be subject to the regulation of more general data protection legislation (for instance, Allan, 2003, cites in the UK the 1998 Data Protection Act). To some extent, national frameworks for data protection have been informed (if not driven) by EU legislation in this area although there is as yet no European-wide convention regarding the ethical aspects of research projects as such.

Virtually all European countries now have at least one professional association for social workers or other social professionals and these are likely to have a code of ethics governing the conduct of social professionals as practitioners (and possibly managers). Similarly, disciplinary associations (for example in psychology and sociology) tend to have codes of ethics guiding their behavior as researchers. What is less likely is that there will be particular codes of ethics (or a section in the general code) relating to the carrying out of research by social professionals (whether as students, academics or practitioner researchers), although some attempt has been made to formulate such a code by educators in the UK (Butler, 2002) and, as mentioned, there is reference to this area in the BASW code.

The establishment of codes of ethics (and even ethical approval for particular projects where universities or other agencies require this) does not necessarily guarantee the sensitive execution of research in the social professional field – which, by definition, is sometimes with people who may be subject to particular forms of discrimination and distress. There might be assumptions that values widely held by social professionals, for example with regard to confidentiality and avoiding causing harm, transfer readily to the social research arena, but clearly there is also a range of ethical issues (such as informed consent, anonymity in presentation of findings) that might be seen as particular to the research environment, and that need more specific attention in the research curriculum (Allan, 2003).

Opportunities for empirical (project) work

Finally, it might be worth considering the arguments for students having the chance to apply their learning through the carrying out of a small-scale research project. While professional training courses in many countries (and certainly postgraduate or post-professional courses) require students to undertake a dissertation (in the UK, or sometimes termed a thesis in other European countries), this may be of a theoretical nature and based solely on a literature review. Alternatively, other courses require students to engage in empirical work, thus facilitating experiential learning about the different stages and challenges entailed in undertaking research.

In the Anglo-American tradition, such a dissertation is often based on project work carried out individually, but Lorenz (2003) has identified the extent to which students on social pedagogy courses in Germany carry out project work in groups (and also suggests that these might have an action orientation in many cases). For many students the main goal of a project becomes the 'findings' and the learning about a social issue or practice dilemma of particular interest to them, but a few become interested in the more general issues associated with research design and implementation, and develop the potential to undertake further research.

An alternative model for learning about research is reflected in the example of a project initiated by a UK former mental health worker who, following a year as a volunteer in the psychiatric field in Bulgaria (Dobrev, 2003), devised a small-scale research project in conjunction with the staff from the local mental health services and the South-West University (Neofit Rilski), Blagoevgrad. During this project, students would be involved in designing an interview schedule and carrying out interviews with the carers of people who had been admitted to a psychiatric hospital, to assess the concerns and needs of carers themselves. Students would undertake these interviews in pairs and also be involved in the data analysis stage and the discussions about the implications of the findings for service development (Wilson, 2004). Such a project demonstrates how students can be enabled to learn about research methods while also supplementing personnel resources in the locality. In addition, students would be engaging with a minority population (people with mental health problems and their carers), which is often neglected or stigmatised, and potentially also making a contribution to attitudinal change and service development locally. While very small scale and localised in its impact, this project seems to reflect both the imaginative use of an external resource person from Western Europe and a sensitive approach to knowledge transfer and capacity building in a country that faces significant challenges adjusting to wider European norms.

As with classroom teaching, it can be questioned whether there are variations in the attention given to ethical issues in agreeing project work in different countries (whether projects are of a comparative nature or not), but anecdotal evidence suggests that ethical concerns may impact on small-scale projects differentially across national borders. One such example occurred in the case of a recent Masters student at the University of East London, UK, who was able to access young asylum seekers in one country (to hear their views about social services available to them) but where access was denied (other than to staff) by an agency in the UK on the grounds that the project had not been approved by an Ethics Committee, thus necessitating a change in the research design. It has since been agreed that all undergraduate and postgraduate students must seek ethical approval from the University at the stage at which they submit project proposals – a practice previously limited to students undertaking research degrees.

Using a comparative framework or European perspective in research

Apart from the role of the EU in funding research programmes specifically, one by-product of the Erasmus, Tempus and later Socrates and related funding initiatives of the European Commission (EC) was the possibility that participants would be able to engage in cross-national or comparative research – or would be able to locate their own (local/national) research in a European context, and it may be useful to consider how far this has happened.

In relation to comparative research – taken to mean research within a common research design and using the same instruments for data collection from comparable samples across at least two countries – this is not an approach that has received much attention in the (English language) social research literature, although there is a useful text by Hantrais and Mangen (1996). But more recently, some important learning about this approach has been identified by authors writing about projects in the social professional field (see, for instance, Hetherington, 1998; Baistow, 2000). So, for instance, a common problem identified relates to the difficulty of translating concepts across countries – this fundamental difficulty then gives rise to technical problems of translating data collection tools, such as questionnaires and interview schedules, into equivalent language. However, with much discussion and negotiation, common tools can be agreed (such as a data collection form for the previously mentioned CERTS Project) or 'new' data collection methods can be devised. (Cross-country analysis of the resulting data in turn enables the conceptual differences to be better understood.) With regard to data collection, some social work research projects have developed the vignette method, in which participants in different countries are presented with the same case scenario and asked about how they (or social workers in their agency or country) would be likely to respond (Froslund et al., 2002; Weytes, 2003).

However, regarding the extent to which such comparative studies have been undertaken in Europe in the social professional field, the results (in terms of published material about the projects) over a 20-year period up to 2000 seem disappointing. Shardlow and Walliss (2003) in a literature review of 285 (English language) publications about empirical research studies, ranging across 42 European countries, found very little evidence of comparative studies. In an initial sweep, 209 out of the 285 articles were rejected as not describing comparative research, and of the remaining 76 publications, 29 were then excluded as constituting policy and statistical literature (that is, being about social welfare policies and trends) and a further 40 were eliminated as providing theoretical or descriptive accounts of social work, rather than including an empirical element.

In the event the authors identified 14 articles as contributing to 'scientific knowledge building' (Shardlow and Walliss, 2003, p. 927) in the social work field (broadly defined). Of these the majority were mainly 'two nation' studies, and, perhaps predictably given the language bias, the UK was one of the countries compared in most cases. Other countries likely to be included in comparative studies were Sweden, France, Italy and Germany, and only in one case, in a study about public attitudes to mental health by Brandon et al. (1998), were there a significant number of countries (eight). The topics of studies ranged across general issues (that is, not client specific – five); child care (four); mental health (three); and social work education (two); and the findings were most often derived from social professionals, with limited voice given to the views of service users. Again, the Brandon et al. study (1998) was alone in its investigation of public perceptions.

With regard to methodology, Shardlow and Walliss (2003) found a slight preference for qualitative methods and identified the use of vignettes or scenarios requiring decisions about 'real-life' situations as important in some cases (for example, Wilford, 1997; Christopherson, 1998). While a number of studies made use of questionnaires, analysis was deemed to be relatively 'simplistic' and in only two studies were data derived from one method triangulated with data obtained by other means (Cooper, 1992; Hume et al., 1998). Unsurprisingly, Shardlow and Walliss concluded that there was significant scope for more (and more sophisticated) comparative research in the social work field and it would be interesting to see whether there has been much change in this situation, if a similar exercise were to be carried out, analysing publications, say, from 2000 to 2005.

One project, current at the time of writing (2004), might give further information about this in due course. The previously mentioned CERTS Project was developed from a previous EU-funded project (also led by ETSUP, 1998–2001), which had identified the national variations in availability of doctoral programmes in the social professional field across Europe and the lack of readily available data (even at national levels) about 'output' of this kind (Laot, 2000). Taken together these two projects have been important in a number of ways, including progressing the debate about the epistemology of social work education and highlighting further the different educational traditions, professional arrangements and assumptions that influence the inclusion of social professionals (including academics) in the research enterprise.

If the CERTS database already established for research outputs across Europe is successfully developed this will offer scope for more systematic analysis of the research topics of most interest to researchers in particular countries, as well as the approaches that have been employed. It will also be possible to see whether researchers attempt comparative research or research that locates policies or practice in a European context. In general, the setting up of a European database should help promote the visibility of doctoral research and establish the basis for increasing knowledge about studies carried out by or relevant to the social professions, as already exists in the US (Lyons, 2003).

Research studies locating national developments within a European framework seem to be even less in evidence but are arguably more likely to be within the competence of solo researchers, particularly where individuals are undertaking postgraduate studies in a different country. The value of these is the extent to which professionals can subsequently develop their own practice locally with enhanced understanding of the European as well as the national context. Potentially, such knowledge contributes to professional performance and can inform service developments, whether locally or across national boundaries. A number of social problems now challenging legislators and a range of professionals (including social workers) are related to global or regional processes and must be addressed from an increased understanding of interrelated causal factors. For instance, issues of particular concern to social professionals in the European context currently include the rise in separated refugee children (Mynott and Humphries, 2002) and the increase in trafficking of people (Manion, 2002). While such issues (and social professional responses to them) can be researched as country-specific 'case studies', they can usefully be linked more explicitly to the socioeconomic conditions elsewhere that give rise to various forms of population mobility and to the European as well as national frameworks that attempt to regulate migration in its various forms.

Conclusion

It can be argued that social professionals, like members of any other discipline and profession, have a responsibility to undertake research or at least to be research minded and employ research findings in professional practice and service development. This has implications for the responsibilities placed on academics in relation to both their educational role and their own involvement in the research process. It has been further suggested that because of the nature of social work and the experience of social professionals in relation to social ills and personal troubles, there is a particular responsibility to undertake (or enable) research that is consistent with professional aims and values. In this respect, research that gives a voice to people who are otherwise disenfranchised or marginalised, and which is carried out in ways that empower service users (as well as promoting their welfare and protecting them from harm) seems particularly appropriate.

Additionally, whether operating in some national contexts or certainly within a European and comparative context, Shardlow and Walliss's (2003) finding, that only a small number of empirical studies seemed to demonstrate cross-cultural sensitivity, should be of particular concern and is an area for more reflection and development. Similarly, there is scope for more inquiry into comparative understandings and practices in relation to the ethics of social research, as well as struggling with the practicalities of undertaking cross-national research (including obtaining funding). On the reverse side, it seems likely that cross-national and comparative research has been made easier by the availability of web-based resources, the establishment of databases and the extensive use of e-mail.

Some of the material cited above lends support to the view that social work education across Europe is undergoing (at different speeds) a period of academisation. As Curry et al. (1993) noted about professional education in the US in the early 1990s (and as was noted in Finland in the 1980s), this might result in an increasing gap between the needs of practice and the forms and foci of research projects. Similarly, Lorenz (2003) has expressed concerns about the developments in Europe and the need for a clear understanding of the meaning and purpose of social work and related research. However, there also seems to be some evidence of an increase in the opportunities for social professionals to learn about research and also to be involved in research projects, whether as solo/practitioner researchers or as part of research teams. Additionally, there are indications that, while research in the social professional field may share similarities with other forms of social research, it might also contribute to developing new approaches in social research, including in the comparative field.

While development of research teaching and carrying out of research by social professionals may have an important role in disciplinary and professional development, it can be argued that its primary goal, when undertaken by social professionals, is to evaluate and improve the services and interventions available to service users. In this respect, there is also considerable scope for the development of approaches and methodologies that empower service users and those engaged in the delivery of social services to participate in knowledge generation and social change. Such approaches include participatory research and action research. In this way, social work research can be seen as an element in the wider European agenda of promoting social inclusion and citizenship, as well as participating in the creation of a European knowledge society.

Chapter 5

Racialised identities: new challenges for Social Work Education

Lena Dominelli

Introduction

Racialised identities and the racist social relations associated with these are key concerns in public life in Western Europe as racial intolerance grows (Cheles et al., 1991; Bjorgo and White, 1993; EUMC, 2005) and the continent tightens its borders, making it harder for non-Europeans to settle in the region whether they enter as (im)migrants, undocumented persons, asylum seekers or refugees. Described as 'Fortress Europe' (Gordon, 1992; Wrench and Solomos, 1996; Back and Nayak, 1998), it has become linked to 'international terrorism' since the attack on the Twin Towers in New York on 11 September 2001.

Consequently, the Fortress has become the armed citadel that is suspicious of those who do not fit the European phenotype within its borders as well as those without. This has produced tendencies to demonise those who cross borders to gain entry, restricted civil liberties for existing citizens, reinvented racial profiling by focusing on cultural symbols such as religion alongside the well-established one of skin colour and yielded what I call 'bio-social racism'.

Across Europe, discourses on asylum seekers and refugees encapsulate responses to (im)migrants generally. They have been redefined in terms of abuse as economic migrants, welfare cheaters, criminals, illegal immigrants and bogus asylum seekers. (Im)migration has also become linked with modern forms of slavery promoted by people smuggling and trafficking associated with forced labour, prostitution, drug trade and organised crime. The numbers trafficked can be substantial, for example, estimates suggest 600,000 women were trafficked between Eastern and Western Europe each year pre-May 2004. Trafficking in people is also a global phenomenon.

In this chapter I examine the shifting nature of 'race' and racialised identities in Western Europe and consider the implications of this development for social work education. Addressing these issues has always been difficult, but contemporary complexities in socio-political relations have made this task much harder.

Rethinking Racialised Identities

Europe, composed of heterogeneous groupings of peoples with diverse languages, cultures, religions and traditions even within individual nation states, has failed to embed valuing diversity as the centrepiece of its yearning for unity. The legacy of colonialism, anti-Semitism including the Holocaust, 'ethnic cleansing', power struggles between different peoples and external searches for resources have impacted strongly on how Europeans perceive themselves. At the same time, there is no singular *European* identity that unifies all. Indeed, if current opinion polls are to be believed, many peoples of Europe preferring their national identities do not wish to acquire one. And others, like the Basques in Spain or Scots in the UK, are trying to separate from the nation state that has sought to absorb them. So, identity remains complicated and unstable at local, national and regional levels.

People's identities are configured through social interactions that are context specific (Giddens, 1990) and reconfigured differently depending on situation and purpose. Identities are complex and develop along many lines, including 'race' gender, age, class, disability, sexual orientation and mental ill-health. People's experiences of racialised identities are differentiated and may simultaneously cover any number of these dimensions, depending on how a person is identified and self-identifies[1]. We should not think of these social divisions as interacting additively with each other, but as intersecting and complicating each other in myriad fluid ways (Dominelli, 2002). Yet, European policy focuses on unitary identity(ies).

'Race' is a socially constructed phenomenon and reflected in our individual and group identities, regardless of who we are and what our location is within a socially ascribed hierarchy of 'race'. We are all racialised. This means that understanding that 'white' Eueopeans are racialised beings is just as important as seeing 'black' Europeans as racialised beings[2]. Crucially, this requires 'white' people to examine 'whiteness' and its often taken-for-granted significance in their lives (Frankenburg, 1997). In racialised societies, 'race' becomes a marker of difference that defines who we are through our interactions with others. It becomes a signifier by drawing on physical and social characteristics such as skin colour, hair texture, religion, social traditions and (re)casting them through a process of differentiation into separate groups that are evaluated differentially. 'Race' both creates the individual or group as a racialised entity and at the same time draws upon individual or group interactions in social relationships to create 'race' as a meaningful category.

As a socially created entity, 'race' involves accepted or hegemonic discourses that take biological or physical attributes and socio-cultural ones and ascribe a particular value to each within a hierarchy of value. These exist in a dyad that delineates which trait is 'superior' and which is 'inferior'. Thus, 'race' becomes a bio-social category in which each feature is ranked in order of desirability to establish a dyad that values 'white' attributes and disparages 'black' ones. I have placed these terms in quotes to emphasise their socially constructed valuing or lack of it, despite some having a biological basis, because judging some as more important than others is a social act.

This binary divide separates people into positive and negative representations of themselves and provides the basis for racist social relations. Institutionalised through social policies, organisational practices and cultural assumptions, 'race' becomes an inherent part of a worldview that people individually and collectively utilise to make sense of their position and that of others, and to structure social relations to achieve particular ends (Dominelli, 2004a). This includes (re)enacting their location as privileged subjects within power relations that configure disadvantaged people as objects of their actions (Dominelli, 2000).

The valuing of particular attributes varies over time as people contest their significance, and so 'race' is a fluid construct that constantly changes form. At the same time, it may remain a fixed entity in some people's perceptions of other people to make 'race' a category that carries both continuity and discontinuities in meaning. Thus, 'race' is created through social interaction and involves *negotiated stances* around people's sense of identity or who they are at both individual and collective levels and is replicated through the routines of everyday life (Dominelli, 2000).

Racialised identities impact upon everyone, including those who are privileged. But, those who are privileged often fail to appreciate that in racialising others, they racialise themselves. The privileging of 'whiteness' within the Western world becomes an assumed or taken-for-granted aspect of life that is seldom commented upon (Frankenburg, 1997). This reinforces the view that racialised identities affect 'other' people, that is, those with dark skins or those who are from different cultures. There is an externalisation of the issue that places the 'other' out there as excluded people while those who are included rise above the fray into a 'race'-less position.

Definitions of 'race' rely on the use of power relations whereby those involved in the interaction seek to impose their worldview on a situation. Power, as Foucault (1980) demonstrated, is multidimensional. Marilyn French (1985) categorises different types of power as power over, power of and power to relations. I have identified how power over others relies on notions of superiority and inferiority to form relations of domination that create people as subordinate beings and underpin relations of oppression (Dominelli, 2002). Hence, oppression involves the abuse of power.

Racism consists of the abuse of power on the basis of 'race' or physical attributes that are taken to signify biological differences between human beings. It becomes a form of social interaction that racialises identities through a binary dyad in which some people's physical and social characteristics are defined as superior and others as inferior. It configures those deemed 'superior' with greater power and privileges than those categorised as 'inferior'. A racist worldview allocates all people into this schema, reserves the privileged category for itself and produces the phenomenon of othering that creates an 'in-group' that occupies the subject position and an 'out-group' that is accorded object status. The 'in-group' privileges itself at the expense of the 'out-group'. Thus, identity becomes both oppositional and relational (Steiner-Khamsi, 2004). Racism involves the dynamics of social inclusion and exclusion, with the former reinforcing racial supremacy, the latter racial oppression.

I define the 'othering' process used in racialising identities as:

an active process of interaction that relies on the creation and re-creation of dyadic social relations in which one group is socially dominant and others are socially subordinate. In 'othering' dynamics, physical or cultural attributes are created as signifiers of interiority through the organisation of social relations in ways that establish this dyadic relationship as the context within which an encounter perpetuates the domination of one group by another. During this interaction, the dominant group is constructed as 'subject' and the oppressed group as 'object'. (see also Dominelli, 2002)

Racism is practised at the personal, institutional and cultural levels (Dominelli, 1988). These three forms of racism are interactive and feed into and off each other and contribute to the complexity of the issue and difficulties in eradicating racist social relations and discourses. As *personal racism*, it draws upon an individual's attitudes and beliefs and behaviour that follow from these. Members of far-right organisations hold personal beliefs that endorse their superior position and act as if others share their views. Sadly, the growth of the far right in Europe has resulted in the mainstreaming of many of their concerns as politicians of other persuasions adopt their messages. Many anti-immigrant sentiments can be traced back to their discourses. And, as they gain greater legitimacy, they set the scene for more restrictive immigration laws and attacks upon foreigners.

Institutional racism in Europe involves legislation, policies and practices that privilege 'whiteness' and guide everyday interactions within formal settings. Laying the basis for what becomes legitimated as acceptable behaviour, these feed both personal and cultural racism. An example is legislation that treats asylum seekers as if they were criminals trying to outwit immigration controls rather than people who fear losing their lives. Institutional racism *others* (im)migrants and recasts them as people without human rights or claims for asylum. As people who do not belong, they can be treated harshly, denied welfare benefits and detained without trial. If they appear at a port of entry without documents, they are deemed to have committed a criminal offence whether or not this is the case, and regardless of whether it was possible for them to procure their identity documents without endangering their lives. Institutional racism often results in indirect racism as a by-product of policy.

Cultural racism highlights the social values and norms that celebrate whiteness and apply to all those living in a particular society. The media are currently recasting European images of immigrants and asylum seekers in derogatory terms – as bogus asylum seekers, welfare abusers and economic migrants. These pictures portray them as *undeserving* claimants and facilitate their being deemed undesirable, lacking the right to stay and appropriately deported to whence they came. In devaluing others, current proposals that those seeking asylum in Europe should be returned to a 'safe third country', kept off-shore while their applications are considered, or allowed to apply to only one country in the European Union (EU), reflect the cultural dimension of racism.

Racism is historically specific. The form perpetrated by 'white' people against 'black' people in Europe has the following characteristics. It:

● racialises identity, particularly ethnicity, while at the same time racialising other aspects of identity, for example, gender is racialised, as is class and other social divisions;
● racialises culture and cultural symbols, for example, religious affiliation;
● essentialises 'race' by focusing on biological relationships and depicting these as natural and immutable, that is, not amenable to change;
● draws on *power over* others to produce racialised relations that privilege the hegemonic or superior group;
● overvalues/celebrates 'white' people's attributes;
● undervalues/pathologises 'black' people's attributes by normalising or treating as most desirable, those characteristics associated with the dominant ('white') group;
● creates unstable social relations because racism has to be constantly reproduced, but also because people's responses to racist social dynamics are complex;
● constantly reproduces racist social dynamics by creating subject-to-object relations and dehumanising those involved;
● rations scarce resources in particular localities through taken-for-granted assumptions that accord these to those enjoying racial privileging before those without it or even at the expense of those considered inferior;
● defines territorial space within an implicit racialised hierarchy, which is articulated as localised possession for the dominant group and thereby maintains as obvious a superior status that does not have to be subjected to explicit evaluation.

The *new* racism identified by Barker (1981) focuses on cultural differences between people. In the UK, this was clearly articulated by Margaret Thatcher during her tenure as Prime Minister when she complained about British culture being 'swamped' by alien ones. This formulation focused explicitly on culture, but she excluded those deemed not British, thereby setting up a dyadic relationship between different cultures that privileged her own unique version of 'white' Britishness as a force that unified a homogenous grouping while excluding 'black' British people, including those born in Britain. She also constructed other cultures in what was officially portrayed as 'multicultural

Britain' as equal but different, thus endorsing a notion of cultural pluralism that promotes cultural relativism while speaking from a position that privileges white British culture. Similar dynamics are evident in other countries, for example, Dutch cultural intolerance as displayed through Pim Fortuyn's List and responses to the murder of Theo Van Gogh.

In formulating culture within discourses of relativism, the new racism assumes that all cultures are equal. Thus, it ignores unequal power relations between different ethnic, cultural or racial groupings. For example, the UK portrays itself as a multicultural society that respects religious difference, but the only religious celebrations that are significant enough to warrant public holidays are those associated with Christianity.

The new racism is undergoing another permutation at the moment in focusing on physical phenotypes such as dark skin and cultural attributes, particularly religion and dress, to give rise to bio-social racism that is being picked up by far-right parties in Europe to exacerbate racial tensions and privilege (primarily Protestant) Christian 'whiteness'. Islamophobia, or the hatred of people following the precepts of Islam, is indicative of bio-social racism and is spreading across the continent.

Racism permeates all aspects of society and is particularly important in controlling the boundaries of the possible or what is doable in society; defining appropriate spheres of influence for different groups; and allocating scarce social resources among privileged groups and individuals through the unquestioned exclusion of those who belong to racially oppressed groups. These boundaries are evident in public and private life and at the points in which people interact with one another to create social relations that reflect status in society, the resources that they can access and their responsibilities vis-a-vis others.

These boundaries are applicable to both dominant and subordinate groups, although the experiences of each group are different. Figure 5.1 depicts how controlling boundaries operate to ensure that people act within socially constituted boundaries in accordance with accepted norms. The three spheres of civil society, household and state are interactive structures with some overlapping areas. Also, there is a small triangle in the middle that indicates the arena in which the three spheres converge.

The state, in mediating between the public and private boundaries is able to influence the relationship between civil society and households through

Figure 5.1: Controlling boundaries

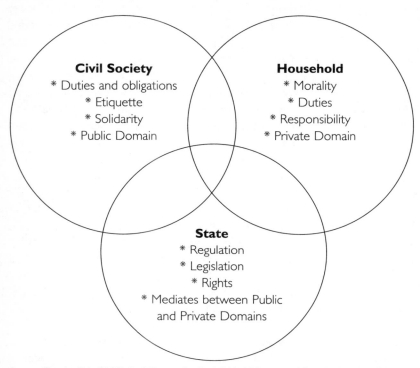

Civil Society
* Duties and obligations
* Etiquette
* Solidarity
* Public Domain

Household
* Morality
* Duties
* Responsibility
* Private Domain

State
* Regulation
* Legislation
* Rights
* Mediates between Public and Private Domains

Source: Dominelli, L (2002) Anti-Oppressive Social Work Theory and Practice London, Palgrave

legislation and policy formation. Consequently, the state has a crucial role to play in either reproducing or eradicating racist relations and establishing the norms that govern acceptable behaviour. The state is subjected simultaneously to pressures from members of both the dominant group and the subordinate one to protect their own specific interests.

In the current configuration of society, the subordinate group's activities occur within the civil society and household levels more than the dominant group's. Although using these to affect what happens within the state's domain, subordinate groups play a lesser role in setting agendas in the public domain despite the state governing social life on behalf of all those living in a particular society. At the same time, it has a considerable degree of freedom in controlling the private sphere of the household in interactions with others from its own social group. As shown later, these dynamics are evident in European governments' handling of racism nationally and regionally through legislation, reports and funding opportunities aimed at tackling racism.

At the individual level, racism involves the dominant group controlling people it deems inferior through the exercise of power over relations. These demonstrate how every aspect of daily life is subjected to relations of control that reinforce power over relations and oppress people on the basis of 'race' (Essed, 1991). These dynamics operate at the emotional, physical and social level to intimidate, isolate and humiliate those at the receiving end of racial oppression. Intergenerational relations are part of this complex. By subjecting relationships between parents and children to controlling relations, racial oppression engenders parental fear of children being attacked for being different and sows discord between generations when their culture becomes a marker of a difference that is disparaged.

Figure 5.2 indicates the complex variety of mechanisms through which this occurs, often within the private sphere in everyday social relations and discourses:

Racist discourses also facilitate the positioning of 'superior' people as those who have *agency* and 'inferior' ones as those who do not and are evident in discourses propagated by far-right parties. In these, the privileged 'race' is accorded *subject* status and the power to act, while the subordinate one is given *object* status or denied the power to act in its own interests. In racist relationships, the interaction creates a subject-to-object relationship that privileges the dominant group (Dominelli, 2000) and is a key dynamic in the construction of 'whiteness' as normative, that is, the entity that contains the attributes whereby all other attributes are judged or valued. This is at variance with egalitarian relationships whereby both groups of participants act as subjects who form *subject-to-subject relationships* in which each exercises agency and negotiates a position that each finds satisfying (Dominelli, 2002).

Exercising agency involves individuals and groups in forming a number of different options from which particular choices are made. The key ones with regards to racist social relations are:

- acceptance;
- accommodation;
- escapism;
- resistance (Dominelli, 2002).

In acceptance options, identity is essentialised and the configuration of social relations in racist terms is taken as given – natural and impervious to change, as is portrayed in far-right ideologies. Only different people are *othered* and

Figure 5.2: Controlling racialised relations

Source: Compiled from: Dominelli, L (2002) Anti-Oppressive Theory and Practice London, Palgrave; Dominelli, L (2004b) Social Work: Theory and Practice for a Changing Profession Cambridge, Polity Press

racialised. Little thought is given to racialised identities of the self, because there is little recognition of this being the case, for example, the fudging of 'white' culture as the reference point in Le Pen's discourses on French culture (see www.frontnational.com/doc_programme.php, accessed 21/07/04) or Nick Griffin's on Britain's (see www.bnp.org.uk, accessed 21/07/04). Acceptance involves internalising the oppressor role if a member of the dominant group, or an oppressed person if a member of the subordinate group. This response can also provide the basis for much indirect racial discrimination where exclusion occurs as a by-product of a particular policy, for example French laws prohibiting obvious displays of religious objects at school. Although including crucifixes alongside headscarves, it ignores the symbolic meaning of these items by decontextualising them. The crucifix is less necessary as a symbol of identity in a predominantly Christian culture than is the headscarf for Muslim women. And, it ignores its gendered implications.

An accommodation formulation of the situation indicates some recognition that a racialisation of identity is occurring, and the attempt to alter it in some way without challenging the overall social arrangement within which people live and interact with others. This may involve making identity more palatable so that people can get on with their lives, or creating small changes in one's perception of others, particularly at the personal level, to make interaction with them easier. This position is adopted by most people who simply want to get on with their lives. They give little thought to 'race' and racism unless it is specifically brought to their notice when interacting with others different from them. This is more likely to occur when people assimilate more readily into the receiving country, such as those from the former Yugoslavia in Italy.

The escapism route involves recognition of the racialised nature of social relations, and their rejection, but without a strategy for either addressing it (as in accommodationist responses) or eradicating it (as in the case of resistance ones). Often feeling disempowered, people choosing escapist ways of dealing with racism believe that the issue is too big for them to deal with and so they will try to avoid it wherever possible and escape into a world of their own making whereby such awful things do not exist. 'White' people using an escapist option in dealing with racism may value 'black' people and include them among their circle of friends, but fail to make connections with either institutional or cultural racism and the personal racism of others that they encounter in their daily lives.

The resistance response involves a rejection of racist social relations and a vision of an alternative way of conducting relationships between different groups of people that is rooted in egalitarian social relations. It also involves a commitment to social change. In this option, 'black' people may choose to work only with other 'black' people to both create and realise their own potential as agents and work towards the eradication of racist social relations. Others may opt to work with 'white' people committed to the same end and seek to establish a racially just society. Neither of these resistance approaches is unproblematic and both can reproduce *power over* relations in which one dominant group is replaced by another, regardless of their ultimate goal, unless specific steps are taken to ensure that egalitarian relationships become the norm. Resistance can also operate within existing legal frameworks to promote 'black' agendas, such as Les Beurs in France.

European Responses to Racism

Europeans have become used to living in pluralistic societies but not necessarily accepting of all who live in them. Assimilation or the expectation that people with origins from other continents or countries should melt into the background by becoming just like the locals has featured prominently in European responses until recently. Europeans struggle with the implications of the multicultural nature of their societies, that is, having many different cultural entities within them. Accommodating diversity and difference remains uncertain and contested as many 'white' European nationals fear the loss of their unique identities and react negatively to others while seeking to maintain the superiority of their position (Bjorgo and White, 1993).

Focusing on the binary of the 'good' and 'bad' foreigner, they justify the call for 'no more foreigners' and vote in significant numbers for far-right parties that promise to resolve these concerns in their favour (Cheles et al., 1991; Bjorgo and White, 1993). These include the Front National in France, Vlams Blok in Belgium, British National Party in England, Freedom Party in Austria, Danish People's Party in Denmark, German People's Union in Germany, Progress Party in Norway, Popular Party in Portugal, Pim Fortuyn's List in the Netherlands and Swiss People's Party in Switzerland. These nationalistic groupings have acquired regional prominence having captured 24 out of 626 seats in the European Parliament and affected social policy.

Expressing racist sentiments is becoming increasingly acceptable as politicians and the media demonise 'foreigners' or 'third-country nationals': 38% of French, 45% of Belgians, 23% of Germans and 22% of Britons describe themselves as racist (Robinson, 2000). The growth of racism and xenophobia in Europe (EUMC, 2005) makes encouraging citizens to live with its increasing diversity in egalitarian ways a key challenge. The association of Islam with terrorism and the murder of high-profile individuals like Van Gogh in Holland have exacerbated this position. This turn of events raises considerable policy-making, practice and educational issues.

Despite the media's demonisation of incomers, the economic case for immigration to Europe is overwhelming. Many countries have declining birth rates and Europe's population is ageing. These demographics reveal that Europe cannot staff its economic enterprises and services without settled (im)migrants accepted as equals. Viewing immigrants as rural, uneducated people is passé. Many are urbanised, highly educated professionals. Abye (2003) has argued that they are already Westernised, being familiar with Western cultures and languages before arrival.

Fortunately, the rise of the far right has been accompanied by the growth of anti-racist initiatives throughout the EU. The European Commission (EC), European Parliament and the Council of Europe (CoE) have various infrastructures for fighting racism. The CoE, founded in 1949 to promote peace on the continent and including 45 countries in the wider Europe, has the European Commission against Racism and Intolerance (ECRI) and a Directorate General of Human Rights (DG II) to combat racism and monitor progress.

Building on the Declaration of 14 May 1981 in which the Committee of Ministers condemned all forms of intolerance, the CoE held the First Summit of Heads of State and governments of the member states of the CoE in Vienna in 1993 and a second one building on this in Strasbourg in 1997. In the Vienna Declaration, 32 member states committed themselves to monitor progress in eradicating racism in individual nation states regularly. In 1993, the Vienna World Conference on Human Rights also created the United Nations Office of the High Commissioner for Human Rights with the goal of promoting and monitoring the struggle against racism.

European Union responses against racism and xenophobia include subscribing to the Vienna Declaration, which identified racism as a violation of human rights in 1993, and legislation at both national and regional levels to guarantee the rights of ethnic and other minorities. From the mid-1990s, the European Parliament considered a CoE (1994) report and subsequent national reports on racism and xenophobia in the EU, declared the European Year Against Racism in 1997, prepared for and participated in the World Conference against Racism in Durban in 2001, and underpinned its initiatives with legislative changes that hinged on defining racist acts as violations of human rights that were deemed universal, indivisible, interrelated and interdependent.

Tackling racist behaviour in the EU received another major boost on 29 June 2000 when Directive 2000/43 endorsing the principle of equal treatment between all peoples was promulgated in Luxembourg. In 2001, the European Monitoring Centre on Racism and Xenophobia (EUMC) in Vienna reported that 64% of EU citizens had positive attitudes towards diversity, although 52% felt that minority groups had a destabilising effect on their polity.

The ECRI's report on each country regularly monitors and reports on the extent to which national initiatives meet regional expectations and directives in tackling racism. Published regularly, ECRI reports highlight national strengths and weaknesses. For example, the 2004 report for the UK applauded the

Immigration and Asylum Act, 1996, for asking employers not to employ undocumented workers and the Immigration and Asylum Act, 1999, for giving guidance to employers in avoiding racial discrimination. However, it criticised restrictive immigration policies, the detention of asylum seekers, the demonisation of immigrants in the media and immigration officers' authority to enter premises, search and arrest people suspected of immigration offences without due process, despite injunctions to the contrary in the Police and Criminal Evidence Act. National reports such as the MacPherson Report (1999) in England have supplemented the ECRI's concerns.

The EU and CoE have also targeted young people and promoted education as central elements in the fight against racism. After the Vienna Summit in 1993, the CoE's Youth Directorate published *Youth Organisations Combating Racism and Xenophobia* to advance this cause. Continuing in this vein, the ECRI and EC's Directorate of Youth and Sport sponsored and funded educational materials, networks, seminars and conferences, for example the 2004 seminar on Islamophobia in Budapest. The Advisory Committee of the Framework Convention for the Protection of National Minorities adds another dimension to the work. The European Committee of Social Rights monitors the non-discrimination elements of the European Social Charter. Those supporting the Charter of European Political Parties for a Non-Racist Society work to further this goal. Also, Ján Figel as Commissioner of Education, Training, Culture and Multilingualism proposed 2007 as the Year of Intercultural Dialogue.

The Organisation for Security and Co-operation in Europe (OSCE) formed in 1975 as the Conference on Security and Co-operation Europe (CSCE) also fosters racial tolerance. It has 55 countries stretching from Vancouver to Vladivostock and a High Commissioner on National Minorities to promote peace and stability in Europe and enhance its role in global affairs by acting as a bridge between East and West.

A wide range of European and international Conventions and protocols (see the Appendix) have relevance for European institutional approaches to addressing and monitoring racism and these articulate with national arrangements. The latter include national legislation that responds to the specific needs of each country and structures for enforcing its provisions, for example, the Commission for Racial Equality in England, the Ombudsman (sic) against Ethnic Discrimination in Sweden, the Parliamentary Commissioner for National and Ethnic Minority Rights in Hungary, and the Rotterdam Charter for policing in a multi-ethnic society in the Netherlands.

International initiatives have been furthered by a range of other ventures. A key one of these has been the appointment of Special Rapporteurs of the UN Commission on Human Rights to monitor individual countries' performance in upholding human rights. These underpin the view that people are global citizens whose rights cannot be violated. The United Nations Education, Scientific and Cultural Organisation (UNESCO) declared 1995 the International Year for Tolerance to promote international consciousness of the issue. And the Visionary Declaration of the World Conference Against Racism in Durban in 2001 affirmed that all peoples on earth constitute one human family and declared diversity as mutually enriching.

Furthermore, non-governmental organisations (NGOs) and civil society also complement national, regional and international initiatives on this front. Non-governmental organisations have set up networks, organisations, campaigns and educational efforts including conferences and seminars to debate the issues, secure support for various initiatives and raise consciousness about racism at local, national and international levels. These include:

● Arbeitskreisgemeinnütziger Jugendaustauschorganisationen (AJA) in Germany, SOS in France;
● European Federation for Intercultural Learning (EFIL);
● Network on Intercultural Learning in Europe (NILE), 14 countries;
● Tolerance and Understanding our Muslim Neighbours (TUM) project involving countries in Eastern and Western Europe, for example, Bulgaria, Germany, France and the UK;
● Forum of Non-Governmental Organisations, End Racism Now.

Non-governmental organisations have also demanded that European and United Nations (UN) bodies eradicate racism and uphold human rights and social justice. Their initiatives have covered mainstreaming the struggle against racism; recognising the role of non-state agents in torturing people; protecting women from gender-specific forms of oppression; preventing the use of children as soldiers; and eradicating punitive approaches to immigration such as carriers' sanctions, visa regimes and safe third-country practices.

European NGOs have linked internationally to argue for the abolition of Third World debt; the elimination of structural inequalities prompted by rapacious forms of capitalist development that ignore the needs of both people and planet earth; reversing the deleterious impact of international financial, trade and health policies on people of African origins; and an end to human rights violations including the use of physically abusive forms of restraints in deporting undocumented (im)migrants.

However, the EU has had difficulties in finding an agreed terminology to encompass the issues involved. Some countries reject the label 'race' and racism, arguing that all people are equal. Others refuse to acknowledge difference as a legitimate basis for inclusion in the nation state, for example France (Abye, 2001). This makes nationalism and racism bedfellows and untangling them a serious challenge (Aluffi-Pentini and Lorenz, 1996). Some celebrate their multiculturalism as the co-existence of different cultures living side by side in peace, for example England. Others have favoured a cultural competence approach, which focuses on people learning about each other's cultural uniqueness, such as the Netherlands. Despite intentions, these approaches have been found wanting: assimilation because it requires people to lose their unique identities; multiculturalism because it posits an insider–outsider dyad that presumes egalitarian power relations and passivity for the 'outsiders'; and cultural competence because it addresses only personal racism (Dominelli, 2004b).

Below, I consider two key approaches in dealing with this issue that are relevant to social work – anti-racist and intercultural initiatives. I do not have space to deal with other approaches to the subject, for example postmodernism or constructionism, but I do focus on two of their key insights – the uniqueness of identity and responding to people as agents who determine their own destiny.

Anti-Racist Social Work

Given that racism is embedded in everyday routines (Essed, 1991), tackling it at that level becomes significant. As social workers are responsible for enhancing people's daily well-being, the question of what social workers can do to challenge racism is important. The answers to it are contested and unfinished. There is little agreement as to what actions would be appropriate in this respect, and multicultural social work, culturally competent social work and anti-racist social work have all been given preference at difference points in time by different groups. While all have merit, all have also been found wanting (Dominelli, 2001).

I will focus briefly on anti-racist social work, which offers more potential for transformative change than the other approaches mentioned because it attempts to deal with both the personal and structural dimensions of racism.

Anti-racist social work is a form of practice that understands the roles that 'race' and racism play in creating racialised social relations in order to oppress people on the basis of socially constructed characteristics or attributes associated with 'race' that produce racialised identities.

Anti-racist social work opposes racist social work or one that endorses racial supremacy and involves movement from a racist society to a non-racist one. It moves on a continuum from racist society to anti-racist society to egalitarian society. It has the ultimate aim of replacing racist social relations with egalitarian ones, celebrating difference and acknowledging the multiple and fluid aspects of identity. Egalitarian relationships are based on the idea that those participating in them act as subjects who negotiate their social realities with one another. It is also part of an anti-oppressive approach to practice that attempts to include the many different dimensions on which oppression occurs (Dominelli, 2002). Anti-racist social work has much in common with 'black' perspectives (Ahmad, 1990) and Africentric perspectives in social work (Jean Baptiste, 2001; Graham, 2002). These celebrate differences between diverse peoples and work towards the elimination of racist social relations.

These three perspectives have commonalities rooted in their common goal of getting rid of racist social relations and producing equality between different racialised groups and working towards a form of social organisation in which 'race' is no longer relevant in allocating resources between people or a barrier in interactions between different groups of people. They also posit some shared identity attributes among those that each seeks to address. Thus, they have been critiqued by postmodernists for 'essentialising' identity. However, I think this misunderstands their position, which is to consider how to struggle against racism – a political act that requires people to come together for a particular purpose on the basis of shared characteristics. This does not detract from the multidimensional or fractured nature of identity. These differences continue to exist, even if they are sent backstage for a period. But a myth about unity is created to achieve a strategic and particular goal.

These three approaches are also different in that 'black' perspectives come out of the experience of being a 'black' person in a predominantly 'white' society and speaking from that standpoint. Africentric approaches are based on having African origins and drawing on well-established African intellectual traditions and contributions to world cultural and social capital. Africentric traditions have been strongly promoted through the works of Asante (1987). These have provided key tenets in developing pride in the scholarship of African intellectual thought and African cultural traditions and advocating their use in social interactions between people. Africentric approaches argue that those in the African diaspora have cultural traditions and norms in common and are useful in enabling African-origined people to survive racist practices including those forms of racial oppression that are enacted in and through social work practice (Jean-Baptiste, 2001; Graham, 2002). Anti-racist approaches encompass all those committed to tackling racism.

The transformative nature of anti-racist approaches, 'black' perspectives and Africentric ones have been problematic for academics, practitioners and policy makers who fear their transformative potential of such approaches and their capacity to reduce the privileging of 'whiteness'. Additionally, some think that these approaches are too totalising to secure the recognition of varied and complex diversities. And so, anti-racist policies and black or Afrocentric perspectives have not found favour across Europe as a whole.

Working to be inclusive across the continent, the EU has recently focused on the idea of interculturalism. Interculturalism keys into the adult education and lifelong learning agendas. It uses education and dialogue across cultures to promote valuing and respecting diversity within a framework of solidarity with others.

Intercultural learning aims to take multiculturalism to the next step by suggesting that different cultures interact with each other and by acknowledging agency. Intercultural learning is a personal growing process and promotes dialogue across difference. Those fostering this approach have secured EU and CoE funding to create networks that develop educational materials, bolstering intercultural learning and supporting harmonious 'race' relations among diverse ethnic groupings within the EU.

The CoE has encouraged intercultural approaches under the slogan 'All different, all equal'. Both the CoE and the EU have targeted young people to counter an alarming increase in their support of racist worldviews. So, youth has become a key agent for change and a range of intercultural educational materials that target them have been produced (see Aluffi-Pentini and Lorenz, 1996; Hazekamp and Popple, 1997). The European Youth Campaign against Racism, Xenophobia, Anti-Semitism and Intolerance is also deeply involved in this work.

Important as interculturalism is, I do not think that it will eradicate European racism. A major reason for this is that the approach presupposes 'whiteness' as a norm and endorses a 'white' worldview. It does not deconstruct 'whiteness' and the privileging associated with it, nor does it grasp the significance and meaning of a 'white' identity for those who support far-right groups. Additionally, it fails to address the diversity of Europe within a 'white' construct that privileges some 'white' peoples above others – particularly Northern Europeans who have white skin, blond hair and blue eyes. And, as the responses to blond, blue-eyed Muslims from the former Yugoslavia or Catholic Poland indicate, they have to be Protestant as well.

The intercultural approach also ignores the embedding of racist practices in the interstices of daily life through which the concept of a particular 'whiteness' is formulated. The so-called 'dark' Europeans of Southern Europe, the Roma/Gypsy communities scattered throughout the continent, the Sinti, and indigenous peoples such as the Sami have a long historical legacy of having their cultures, languages, religions and traditions deemed inferior and disparaged. Recent moves in this vein include the tenets of the Lega del Norde in Italy, the blood rule to claim German ethnicity in Germany, or the removal of Gypsy children from their parents and denial of their heritage in Switzerland. Additionally, a consideration of intercultural learning materials indicates that other social divisions such as gender, class, age, disability and sexual orientation and their interaction with 'race' are treated only cursorily. Additionally, the casting of racialised identities in binary dyads of superiority and inferiority is not undone by intercultural learning.

Also, the structural causes of migration including poverty and underdevelopment across the world are not fully incorporated in intercultural approaches. Globalisation and neo-liberalism have undermined the capacity of people to look after their own needs in their countries of origin. International trade and debt exacerbate existing economic inequalities as the gap between rich and poor widens (Wichterich, 2000). These are macro-level political issues that need a different kind of politics for their aim of an egalitarian society to be realised. Intercultural learning can make a moral case for pursuing such ends, but cannot deliver them. In focusing on personal growth, it neither seeks to do so nor to consider their relevance to the broader political agenda.

New Steps for Social Work Education

Focusing on racialised identities is an important addition to strategies for tackling racism in all its forms. People can more readily become engaged in the process of doing so by understanding who they are personally and how the racialisation of social relations affects them as well as others. In Dominelli

(1995) I developed a model that I have found useful in helping students begin this process by focusing on their own individual agendas to find out what 'race' has meant to them personally and helping them to unpack their own racialised identities. In this way, they have learnt how racialised identities have impacted upon their relationships with both those who are like them and those who are different from them, covering other social divisions such as gender, sexual orientation and class in the process.

Only after working on these concerns did I encourage students to move on to consider working on developing anti-racist practice in social work. This was subsequently undertaken in the context of mixed teams, which included people from other ethnic and racial groupings to simulate the kinds of situations that they would encounter in daily professional practice. The contextualisation of their work meant that theory, practice, historical conjuncture, legal frameworks, organisational climate, socioeconomic formations and political climate became an inherent part of their problem-solving endeavours. Thus, structural inequalities and consideration of how to overcome them became incorporated as an integral aspect of the model.

The implications of this analysis for social work education are considerable and raise issues that social work educators and practitioners need to take into account in preparing students for anti-racist practice (Dominelli, 1995). These are:

- providing courses that enable students to understand 'race' as a social construct;
- providing courses that enable students to understand the dynamics of racism and the historical contexts within which particular types of racism are (re)formed and altered;
- enabling students to explore and value difference and diversity;
- enabling students to explore and situate themselves as racialised beings'
- enabling students to understand how their persona as individuals interacts with their structural position(s) in society, on the course, in social work practice;
- enabling students to discuss their fears/anxieties in dealing with racism;
- ensuring that analyses of 'race' and racism permeate the entire curriculum in both the field and the academy;
- providing models of good anti-racist social work teaching and practice;
- ensuring that the practice placement or fieldwork experience is one that also teaches students about anti-racist practice and trains them in its effective use;

- developing good relationships between the academy, practitioners and community groups that represent different ethnic groupings and involving them in the teaching of anti-racist models of practice;
- dialoguing with policy makers and other professionals to ensure that they also understand and support anti-racist social work;
- transforming existing social relations and restructuring them in egalitarian directions that will promote human rights and social justice.

Conclusion

Racialised identities are part of daily social realities whether people belong to a minority or a majority ethnic grouping and are socially constructed through social interactions among people. Their presence within the social landscape of contemporary Europe is a source of injustice and oppression. Racist social relationships have to be eradicated in favour of egalitarian relations that use solidarity, connectedness and interdependence to create each person or group as a subject. Social work educators and practitioners involved in transforming racist social relations into egalitarian ones have to enact a developmental approach to their work and be capable of linking what happens in rich countries located mainly in the Northern Hemisphere to what happens in poor countries positioned primarily in the Southern Hemisphere (Midgley, 1997). They also have to be committed to ensuring that social work practice does not become another way of creating imperialist or neo-colonialist relations (Flem, 2004). These concerns are incorporated in the desire to produce a sustainable development that protects the earth's physical environment alongside promoting the economic, political, social and spiritual growth of its peoples (Dominelli, 2002, 2004a). Realising this goal presents social workers with a challenging agenda.

Note

1 This chapter draws on the third edition of *Anti-Racist Social Work* by Lena Dominelli, which is due to be published by Palgrave in 2005.

2 I use 'white' people and 'black' people as political terms signifying those who benefit from racism in Europe and those disparaged and disadvantaged by it respectively and not as identity categories.

Part 3

Learning from Experience

Chapter 6

Europe and the Undergraduate Programme
Kieron Hatton

Introduction

The accession of 10 new countries to the European Union (EU) in 2004 throws an important light on the contribution social work can make to promoting social solidarity, social cohesion and equality. However, at the same time it draws attention to the way social work's commitment to social justice and empowerment exposes the different ways in which states treat their citizens. Social work becomes a paradigm of the way societies can transform or transmogrify. How then can we learn from each other so that our practice becomes transformative and liberatory rather than part of the structures of oppression many social work service users face on a day-to-day level? One way in which this can happen is for social workers to learn from each other, to reject narrow national specifications of their role and to embrace the knowledge, skills and experience of other countries.

In this changing environment it is not surprising that a number of higher education institutions have developed programmes with other European countries. In the UK, two-day conferences organised by the International Sub-committee of the Joint University Council Social Work Education Committee (in 2002 and 2003) focused on how research expertise and undergraduate and postgraduate training programmes have sought to equip students with knowledge and skills about the international (particularly European) framework within which social work is practised. More broadly, the ECSPRESS network, supported by the EU, sought to share ideas about best practice and the latest theoretical developments among a wide group of social professionals (Seibel and Lorenz, 1998; Chytil and Seibel, 1999). The evaluation of the impact of Erasmus on the social professions identified three different models of 'Europeanisation' evident at undergraduate and/or postgraduate levels (Lyons, 1999c). These were the inclusion of European units or modules, often as options in (mainly) undergraduate programmes; the joint development of special (additional) multilateral short courses (usually on the basis of funding for intensive seminars and also mainly in relation to undergraduates); and finally the collaborative development of whole award-bearing courses or programmes.

The experience of offering a joint training programme (at undergraduate level), between social work schools in England and Denmark, provides an insight into how this process of intercultural communication may occur and is used in this chapter to illustrate some of the learning arising from this experience. The BA European Social Work (hereafter BA ESW) degree was initiated by the University of Portsmouth initially (from 1992) in partnership with Skovtofte Seminarium in Copenhagen. This programme is now run in conjunction with Frobel seminariat in Copenhagen, and has also developed links with Pieksammaki Diaconia Polytechnic in Finland and Oslo College in Norway. The programme runs from August to the following June and is taught jointly in both Denmark and England. The students are recruited from a wide range of European countries (to date, Denmark, Sweden, Germany, Spain, Finland and Norway) and (in 2003 and 2004) from Kenya. Between 1992 and 2000 approximately 70-80 students attended the programme from the UK[1].

To reflect the different academic and practice traditions across the two countries delivering the teaching (Denmark and the UK), the course has been designed to incorporate the best of both traditions. The course has therefore included teaching aimed at reflecting the UK concern with diversity and difference and the Danish concern to promote solidarity and equality (Hatton, 2001).

Lack of material initially hindered the development of the academic content of the course, although this was subsequently partially remedied by the development of the journals *Social Work in Europe* and the *European Journal of Social Work* plus the work of the ECSPRESS project (Chytil and Seibel, 1999). However, the course team also made considerable progress in developing collaborative teaching and, as discussed below, the programme now raises substantial theoretical and practice issues that can make a significant contribution to the gaps identified by Shardlow and Walliss (2003) in terms of the development of new areas of empirical research and in ensuring that 'a wider range of countries and a wider range of 'voices' are heard' (p. 938).

Context: The internationalisation of education

Previous chapters have highlighted how the internationalisation of higher education has proceeded apace during the last 10 years. Van Der Wende (2001) points to a generally positive view of the developing international agenda in higher education and suggests that 'the academic rationale (quality improvement) and the development of a European dimension are still very important arguments for internationalisation policies in Europe' (p. 434). He pointed to the importance of the Bologna agreement (see Chapters 2 and 3) in further promoting European perspectives and the process of student mobility. It seems likely that this process will lead to harmonisation of the length of undergraduate courses, and, for instance, the move to three-year social work degree programmes in the UK and discussions about shortening social work training from four years to three in Belgium, also suggest that this will impact on the social professions as much as other subjects. Such harmonisation may make the running of joint courses or modules potentially easier, with students being at the same stage in their education and training programmes.

Kristensen (2001) argues that transnational mobility can promote labour market mobility (see Chapter 8), through fostering a kind of 'transnational consciousness' and suggests that work placements can be promoted as a tool for 'fostering skills in the participants, notably international (foreign language proficiency, intercultural competence) and personal (broad generic skills)' (Kristensen, 2001, p. 423). He also suggests that the development of intercultural competence and the provision of contrasting work experience can be important in fostering personal skills. He sees this as occurring through two processes: immersion and responsibilisation. Immersion he defines as 'the degree of proximity to and interaction with another culture and mentality' (p. 248). Responsibilisation denotes, he suggests, 'the space that is available to the participant for autonomous decision-making in their living and working environments' (p. 248). To achieve these processes he calls for programmes to develop methods for 'preparation, supervision (mentoring) and de-briefing of participants in mobility activities' (p. 428). These were issues pertinent to the BA ESW and they are returned to below.

However, it is worth remembering that international education, particularly in the social professions, is not just about instrumental and/or work-based goals; it is often related more to 'broadening the knowledge and attitudinal base from which future practice (wherever it may take place) will be informed' (Lyons, 1999a, p. 27). She points to the importance of international social work education as 'offering the possibility of developing new paradigms of intervention and enhancing understanding of cultural difference and structural oppression' (p. 29). These are among the issues raised by the development of the Portsmouth–Frobel programme and they will be addressed below.

History and structure of BA European Social Work

Lyons (1998) suggested that there were three models of European training for the social professions: multi-lateral seminars; (common) 'European' modules; and courses leading to academic awards. The Portsmouth–Frobel programme fits the last model. The BA ESW commenced in 1992 following planning between the University of Portsmouth (UK) and Skovtotke Seminarium in Virum (a suburb of Copenhagen). It was agreed that the course would deliver a programme of undergraduate education to students from a range of social welfare backgrounds. Initially the programme was available to students from the two countries (12 from each) who were studying for a qualification in social pedagogy in Denmark and who had completed a UK Diploma in Social Work. In the 1990s the UK qualification was two years and the Danish qualification three years, so the programme was offered to students in either the last year of training in Denmark or immediately after professional qualification in the UK.[2]

At that time a major difference in the educational systems was the length of the study programme. In Denmark the course of study to become a qualified social pedagogue is three years. The Danish programme is determined by the Ministry of Education, although the 32 colleges offering the programme can decide exactly how it should operate within the parameters set. In England up until 2003 the professional qualifying programme was two years. It was also heavily regulated by the accrediting body (formerly the Central Council for Education and Training in Social Work – CCETSW), although there has been some change with the move to a new degree and regulation by the General Social Care Council (GSCC).

Forty-five per cent of the Danish programme emphasises personal development in skills and knowledge across a broad range of creative activities. This reflects the working environment and relationship pedagogues seek with service users of the social services, as well as the other settings – kindergartens and nurseries – in which pedagogues also work. This detail is important as it demonstrates a significant difference between the work of a social worker in the UK and a pedagogue in Denmark.

Initially students coming from the UK to join the BA ESW programme already possessed a recognised social work qualification. The focus of their studies was the legal framework, policy dimensions of social welfare, and a value base rooted in an understanding of social exclusion. The student must have demonstrated the acquisition of the core competencies laid down by CCETSW by the completion of the two-year programme. So for a decade, students from the two main participating countries were at different stages in their professional qualifying training.

Table 6.1 Pathway to qualification for BA ESW students

Country	Number of years	BA ESW	Outcome
Denmark	2	1	BA ESW + a further 6 months of training for Denmark qualification
UK	2 (DipSW)	1	Professional qualification + BA ESW
Norway	2	1	Professional qualification in social work/social practice
Finland	2	1	Professional qualification in social work/social practice

Source: Sears and Brobeck (2003)

This clearly has implications for the level of understanding and critical thinking that students bring to the programme. However, the programme seeks to minimise the effect of these differences in pathways to qualification by drawing on material and teaching from the other participating countries (see below for a discussion of the way Danish and UK theoretical and practice traditions have been utilised).

As mentioned, the programme was designed to reflect the different academic and practice traditions of each country. The first term was taught in Copenhagen and involved the students in mixed study groups researching and presenting a topic on comparative social work (social pedagogy and social care in Europe). A UK tutor spent a week teaching anti-discriminatory theory and practice and the students were expected to incorporate such a perspective in all assessments throughout the course (see below for a fuller discussion of the assessment strategies used on the programme). The presentations were of approximately two-and-a-half hours and the students were expected to draw on theory and practice from other countries. During this term the students also attended a residential event where they were encouraged to discuss their feelings about studying in another country and their participation in an international programme. The students were also expected to participate in a range of cultural and artistic activities and, where possible, to use these skills in their presentations (see discussion below of common-third and problem-based project work). At the end of the first term the students were then expected to produce a reflective account of their learning during that period, focusing on what they had learned about social work values internationally and the divergent trends in international/European social work.

During the second term the students are placed in social work agencies. The Danish students travel to Portsmouth and undertake placements with a wide range of welfare agencies ranging from social services child care teams to community-based mental health services and local voluntary agencies such as homelessness projects, advocacy projects, and community safety partnerships. The UK students stayed in Copenhagen and undertook placements in a similarly wide range of projects – including Open Door, a project for people experiencing violence within the home; Kofode Skole, a homelessness project that seeks to integrate homeless people back into the labour market (Anders Dropping et al., 1999); various Red Cross projects working with asylum seekers; a centre for people with learning disabilities; and a number of residential projects for young people living away from home. The students undertook a study of their placement agency and were asked to evaluate the potential of the agency's methods of intervention for practice in their own country.

In the third term (conducted in Portsmouth), when all the students came back to university after their placement experience, they individually undertook an extended study/dissertation around an area of social work theory and practice. The students were also expected to make an oral presentation on an issue they had not covered previously in one of their assignments. Concurrently, the students received training in research methods with a particular focus on comparative research.

The students were therefore subject to a wide range of assessment methods although the final degree qualification offered was accredited by the University of Portsmouth. This presented a potential problem for the programme as it would have been easy for the university to impose an Anglo-centric approach to learning and to minimise the importance of pedagogic and androgogic traditions in other countries, leading to what Cornwall (1994) has called 'cultural colonisation', where the methods of one country are seen as intrinsically 'better' or more systematic than those found in other countries.

Efforts to avoid cultural colonisation were made by developing the curriculum together and ensuring that the Danish approach to education was as fully reflected in the teaching and assessment as more commonly found approaches in the UK. Consequently the international group-work assignment and reflective review in Copenhagen were given the same weighting as the more traditional academic assignment required in Portsmouth. This was also reflected in 2002 when the programme was unitised and the academic credit for each part of the degree was designated to ensure the equal validity of all aspects of the programme. (The current credit weighting is outlined in Table 6.2). The programme is taught in English and this means that the responsibility for assessment lies disproportionately with the UK teaching team although as much assessment as possible is conducted jointly – for instance, British tutors travel to Denmark for the international group-work presentations (social pedagogy and social care in Europe) and Danish tutors travel to the UK for the individual oral presentations (frameworks of comparison). This at least goes some way to meet the requirement that course staff have the

> ... flexibility to incorporate each culture's (and subculture's) own methodologies of support ... to focus on individual strengths and the structural (organisational, community, political) changes which can support and mobilise these strengths ... (which) ... can be particularly useful for social work in an international context by virtue of its concentration on people's capacity to live in the face of seemingly overwhelming adversity. (Taylor, 1999, p. 317)

This is a useful reminder of the importance of cultural sensitivity and the need to link micro and macro analysis if we are to achieve an international understanding of possible ways forward.

Table 6.2 Units offered on BA ESW and distribution of credits

Unit title	Location	Credit	ECTS	Assessment method	Assessment responsibility
Social pedagogy and social care in Europe	Copenhagen	50	25	International group work and presentation	Joint
International dimensions of oppression	Copenhagen	10	5	Reflective review	Joint
Practice in international context	Portsmouth/ Copenhagen	10	5	Placement agency study	Portsmouth or Copenhagen
Frameworks of comparison	Portsmouth	10	5	Oral presentation	Joint
Research methods (only offered since 2002)	Portsmouth	10	5	Research proposal	Portsmouth
Dissertation	Portsmouth	30	15	Dissertation 10-15,000 words	Primarily Portsmouth but Copenhagen where student expresses preference

Note: ECTS=European Credit Transfer Scheme.

Reflections on the Danish/UK collaboration

Running a programme such as that outlined above raises a number of complex issues both for future collaboration within this programme but also for collaborative arrangements more generally. These include the issues of intercultural communication, the values underpinning social work, the different methodologies adopted (particularly the link to different traditions such as pedagogy), the different practice environments within which students operate, the assessment strategies devised and the resource implications of such collaborations.

Intercultural communication

The term intercultural communication refers not only to the very basic matter of linguistic differences, but also to different interpretations of the world stemming from different social, economic, political and philosophical viewpoints. This raises important issues about how we interpret each other's thoughts and meanings. How do values – that appear to provide a common currency in terms such as empowerment, equality and anti-discrimination – play out in collaborative exchanges? The previous discussion about the internationalisation of education assists our appreciation of this area.

Young suggests that 'the internationalisation of education presents great opportunities for growth in international understanding' (Young, 1996, p. 176). He points to the need not to essentialise or absolutise a particular culture or 'we run the risk of losing our humanity to it. Members of all cultures have some possibility of autonomy in respect of them and it is this that makes it possible for them to see the possibility of intercultural spaces' (p. 208). The search for these spaces leads us to an intercultural action, which in turn allows us to form intercultural relationships in which we can ensure 'the appropriate balancing of the need for common ground with the need to recognise difference' (p. 209; see also Havrdova, 1998; Hatton, 2001; Berry et al., 2002).

This highlights an important element in intercultural communication – the notion of power. Foucault has described how an individual's power is framed through a dialectical process in which 'they are always in a position of simultaneously undergoing and exercising ... power. They are not only its inert or consenting target; they are always also the elements of its articulation' (Gordon, 1980, p. 98). The social actor, the service user, should therefore be at the centre of the discussions about international social work and cultural difference at the centre of our discourses on how we can work together. As Robinson comments, 'power is an important variable in an interethnic communication situation': power is linked to racism in the sense that power provides those elevated to the 'superior position with the ability to carry out their perceptions and role definitions' (Robinson, 1998, p. 142). Robinson is writing about the way counselling and social work fail to understand the needs of Black groups who use services. However, what she says also has resonance for all engaged in international education. As well as mutual respect between international colleagues, students need to be valued for the contribution they can bring to our exchanges. UK universities are often in a powerful position relative to other countries because of the size and influence of the institutions within which social work educators work compared to those of some international colleagues[3]. We therefore need to be aware that we do not seek to privilege British understanding and traditions in the educational experiences we are trying to create. As Lorenz says, 'Intercultural competence is the skill to sustain the tension between difference and equality and to give it political validity. It therefore is a central set of skills in the context of contested and often confused notions of identity in a globalising society' (Lorenz, 2002, pp. 13–14).

Methodological and theoretical issues

One of the key challenges faced when establishing the BA ESW was that while many staff were well versed in the methodology, knowledge base and values underpinning UK social work, knowledge of European traditions was much less developed. This was particularly true of pedagogy, a tradition that had received little exposure in the UK other than through the work of Hadyn Davies Jones (and initially this was available in Danish rather than English – see Coutioux et al., 1984; and later Cannan et al., 1992). It is easy to underestimate the lack of contact between UK and European traditions in social work especially since the concept of pedagogy has received more exposure over the last few years (Higham, 2001; Boddy et al., 2003; Petrie, 2004).

Petrie (2003) has written about how pedagogy can be rendered invisible through the process of translation as its most obvious translation is as 'education', and pedagogues therefore appear as teachers. While there is undoubtedly an element of education in pedagogy it seems more useful to see the concept as one that can inform the practice of social professionals. To 'the whole domain of social responsibility for children, for their well being, learning and competence ... the use of the term pedagogy allows for a discourse that can rise above differences based on, for example, the age of those who use services or a service's immediate goals; it permits any particular provision to be located in the context of a wider social policy towards children' (Petrie, 2003, p. 13). Elsewhere Petrie describes pedagogy as person-centred – 'head, hands and heart – all three being essential for the work of pedagogy' (Petrie, 2004, p. 4). Petrie and colleagues suggest that pedagogic training could usefully be incorporated into UK work with children, particularly looked-after children (Boddy et al., 2003; Petrie, 2004).

Experience on the Portsmouth programme indicates that pedagogy is used much more widely than only in relation to child care. In Denmark, pedagogues are employed to work in residential and day care settings, as part of multidisciplinary teams (often with psychologists, social ardgivers[4] and health workers) and in initiatives such as the social services, school and police (SSP) projects (for example, Blaeksprutten in Copenhagen). However, it is undoubtedly true that pedagogy can make a real difference to current UK thinking about social work, both in terms of values and the theories underpinning practice (Hatton, 2001).

Pedagogy has many elements in it and can be said to be influenced by a diverse range of philosophies and theories from Kierkegaard to Freire to social constructionism. Higham (2001) has suggested that pedagogy is rooted in humanistic principles, arguing that social pedagogy, 'promotes well-being through broadly based educational activities ... (and) ... prevents social problems by empowering people with knowledge and skills to manage their lives' (Higham, 2001, p. 25). Clearly such an approach draws on Freirian ideas about 'conscientization' (Freire, 1972), particularly where Freire talks about the need for dialogue, deindividualisation and critical thinking.

Two key ideas stand out from the pedagogic traditions adopted by our colleagues in Copenhagen – the idea of the common-third and problem-based project work[5].

The 'common third'

This is an idea that has not been widely explored within debates around the work of the social professions but which is used fairly widely within Danish pedagogy. Aabro (2004) describes the 'common third' as a descriptive project or ambition within the pedagogical tradition of 'relations in social work' in which there is a 'deliberate focus on the object as something outside the subject'. The object being a 'common thing' with which both in the relationship can connect. Husen describes this process as: 'to be sharing something, to have something in common, implies in principle to be equal, to be two (or more) individuals on equal terms, with equal rights and dignity (subject–subject relation). In a community you don't use or exploit the other (subject–object relation)' (Husen, cited in Pĕcseli, 1996, p. 231, translated by Aabro, 2004).

At the core of this relationship are notions of equality and respect and the eradication of unequal power relations. As Aabro (2004) suggests, 'through a common or joint activity the users and the social workers enter a subject–subject relation ... (in which) ... the professional is meant to 'forget himself' and the things around him – and devote entirely to the process and activity ... the pedagogical challenge is to be able to realise activities which don't reflect the interests and needs of only one part, but instead seek to establish a *common* and *productive* activity' (emphasis in original). Lihme suggests that this relationship defines the social pedagogical approach as special because 'in the work with the child, unlike therapy, is the perspective of 'action', better known as the 'common third', where social workers and children/young adults meet through a common potential of learning, on a basis of activity and action' (Lihme, 2004, p. 181 cited in Ritchie, 2004, translation by Aabro, 2004).

Borghill (2004), a student on the BA ESW during the academic year 2003/04, described this process well in her undergraduate dissertation:

> The method involves pedagogues and service users concentrating on an activity together e.g. sports, repairing a car, or making a film, virtually anything. The point is that both the pedagogue and the service users have to be genuinely interested in the activity. This way their relation is moved to the background and does not seem important anymore. They are working towards a common goal, which is meaningful to all participants.

> The activity has to be seen as a whole process where the service users are involved as equals in all phases, which are: choosing the activity, planning how to carry it out, actually doing it and in the end appreciating the result and evaluating the process. The young people must be given responsibility and the possibility to use their potential. According to Husen this should strengthen the young person's self-confidence and identity and at the same time working together with other people requires social and communicative abilities such as understanding, cooperation and respect for the opinions of others and these skills will be developed. (Borghill, 2004, p. 16)

Problem-based project work

Problem-based project work has been a key element of pedagogical education in Denmark since the 1980s. Drawing on the work of critical theorists from within the Frankfurt School, the liberation pedagogy of Freire and the experiential-based learning of Piaget, a model was developed, which comprised 'a combination of political and critical intentions and a learning theory that argued for the importance of student activity as opposed to blackboard activity' (Prins, 2004, personal communication). Berthelsen et al. (1996) define this approach as a

> Pedagogical mode of study, where students – in cooperation with teachers and sometimes others – explore and deal with one or several problems closely related to the way in which the problems appear. This implies that the project work is to provide an ever stronger experience, more profound knowledge and a broadened perspective; that the problems are confronted and dealt with from different angles, free from the traditional subject borders, and that the choice of theories, methodologies and tools are linked directly to the choice of a problem. The role of the teacher is no longer only to provide knowledge, but also in solidarity with the students to work as motivator, facilitator, supervisor, and consultant. The project work is concluded in a product which can be a report/paper, or be expressed through other media or concrete actions. (Berthelsen et al., 1996, p. 23, translation by Prins, 2004).

Prins (2004) argues that this is consistent with the educational principles at the Frobel Seminariet, which focus on 'how to enable students engage in empowering, professional relations and thereby facilitate development in other people's lives. The ideal is self-reliant responsible social workers, who are able to question their reality in a critical way and search for knowledge, understanding and solutions'. (See discussion below of assessment strategies as an example of how to actualise these principles.).

Clearly there are points of connection between the theories, principles and values underpinning both Danish and UK social work. The focus on equality, respect and student-centred learning are central to both traditions. They provide a means of focusing or refocusing social work on its humanist goals rather than the technocratic welfarism (Dominelli and Hoogvelt, 1996) currently being promoted in the UK through the competency models favoured by regulatory and funding bodies.

We can learn from these different theoretical approaches so that, as the author has argued elsewhere, we can meet the challenge to remain 'rooted' in our own understandings but be prepared to shift sufficiently ... (so that) ... each others contributions are respected while retaining a belief in the validity of our own contribution' (Hatton, 2001, p. 277).

The points of connection are highlighted in Table 6.3.

Table 6.3 Learning from each other

Country	Theory	Practice	Values
Denmark	Pedagogy: Common-third Problem-based project work	Empowering, Promoting equality, Allowing risk, Sharing/ enabling	Equality, Respect, Dignity, Solidarity, Humanism
UK (recognising the diversity of the UK particularly following devolution)	Person-centred, Case management Residual, Progressive work in community	From individualistic, risk minimisation case work to community development	Anti-discriminatory, Promotion of difference, Empowering, Humanism

Assessment Strategies

The assessment of students on social work programmes takes many forms, including written papers, continuous assessment, group work, presentations, case studies and examinations. Increasingly, social work programmes have recognised the importance of diversity and difference in the delivery of training and have tried to ensure that the training offered equips the student to recognise the personal, institutional and structural factors impacting on the experience both of the students in training and of the service users with whom they work. From a relatively narrow focus on race and gender in the UK in the 1980s, most educational and training providers now focus on the wide range of oppressions that people face in a post-modern and post-colonial society, related to age, sexual orientation, disability, ethnicity and (less often) class. Even allowing for the continuing lack of attention given to linguistic and national discrimination (for example against Welsh, Irish and Scottish people in the UK), social work's primary paradigm is one of inclusion and empowerment.

In relation to assessment in social work practice, Fook (2002) has commented on how we need to be aware of the limitations of traditional approaches and avoid using fixed categories, identities or formulations of power relationships. She says that there is a need to problematise the process of assessment so that the voice of the service user is heard within it. These are issues that have become highlighted in European exchanges where the assessment process impacts both on the student and on the forms of intervention the student is expected to undertake. It is therefore important to formulate in our own practice mechanisms of assessment that are culturally sensitive and culturally equivalent. Cultural sensitivity can be achieved by developing an 'understanding and acceptance of one's own culture in relationship to the culture of others' (Sakina Mama, 2001, p. 374). Cultural equivalence refers to the different expectations placed on 'exchange' students by their own institution and their host institution (De Vita, 2002). Staff have tried to address both of these issues in designing the assessments within the BA ESW programme and to be sensitive to the different academic and theoretical traditions. There has been a recognition that international students are sometimes more comfortable with different forms of assessment other than the individualised models generally found in UK social work.

This approach is exemplified by the unit studied at the beginning of the course, (while in Denmark) – social pedagogy and social care in Europe. The unit is taught over the first term. The students are expected to work in international groups to develop a two-and-a-half-hour presentation about an issue pertinent to European or international social work. Each student is expected to bring, or acquire, information about their own country and they are expected to use a comparative and anti-discriminatory framework to look at the commonalities and differences in the practice area they are examining. The groups are facilitated by a Danish tutor with support visits from UK tutors to provide teaching input around anti-discrimination/anti-oppression, comparative welfare, research methodology, social work theory and practice and social policy.

The unit aims to equip the student to:

● critically reflect on and build on prior professional education and training to develop an independent and systematic approach to the course work;

- generate a critical understanding of contemporary social divisions and social issues from a comparative analysis of different societal contexts;
- develop a critical understanding of social work and social welfare within an international perspective;
- develop skills in group and project work;
- demonstrate a common understanding of key concepts in social work and social pedagogy.

Central to the teaching has been the use of the 'Skovtofte method' – a group-work approach that encourages the students to be critical and reflective of their practice while encouraging in them a respect for the differnt national and international traditions represented within the group (see discussion of problem-based project work above). In addition to the informal knowledge transfers that occur in groups, this method enables the students to develop a broader range of skills than those found within the social work curriculum in the UK. While interpersonal, intrapersonal and interorganisational skills remain important, the students are expected to use a wide range of creative and artistic skills, both to facilitate their learning and in their final presentations. Students spend a period during each week developing this creative side of their skills repetoire, whether it be learning a musical instrument, learning a practical skill or engaging in drama. Such an approach is central to the idea of the 'common third' where the social worker/pedagogue and the the the service user are each expected to bring something to their relationship so that they can create something together equally (as discussed).

Such a broadly based unit clearly provides challenges within the assessment process. Within the one-year programme this unit attracts 50 academic credits – a considerable proportion of the 120 credits the students are expected to gain at level 3 (for the award of the BA). When this unit was first designed, all students were awarded the same mark for the presentation so that the group-work process was not marred by a competetive ethos. However, subsequently the assessment was changed to reflect individual contributions (30%) and group contributions (70%). This proved problematic as it failed to acknowledge the individual performance of the student sufficiently clearly to ensure that the contribution of each student was properly acknowledged.

This has made the assessment more difficult. For each of these factors the student's contribution to the group process needs to be assessed (by the group facilitator) as well as their input into the group presentation at the group presentation by the international tutors. This change to the assessment of the unit more accurately reflected individual contributions (thus allowing staff to fit within the UK assessment framework) and group contributions (being more reflective of Danish and Scandinavian academic traditions). However, the weighting of the individual and group elements of the presentation did not fully recognise the contribution of each student and staff have now introduced a further change to allow students to gain 50% for each element.

This mode of assesment can have important implications for debates about assessment. In particular it suggests opportunities for innovation and creativity if:

● assessment, as well as teaching, is based on intercultural understanding so that UK/US assessment models are not imposed on students, practitioners and service users, who come from more varied educational and cultural backgrounds than UK current assessment methods allow for;
● any review of assessment methods can be used to learn from other countries and move away from the mechanistic and technical views of knowledge construction we commonly use to explore new ways of learning and assessing learning;
● colleagues and students can be encouraged to look beyond the UK/US paradigms to learn from the diverse and exciting theories and practices avaliable in Europe.

Practice Opportunities

One of the major challenges in developing a collaborative European programme is to ensure that the student can explore the ideas that underpin social work in each country. The most useful way of doing this is to place students in practice opportunities that demonstrate to them the different ways in which welfare practice operates in each country. It is also highlights some of the issues raised by Kristensen with respect to the efficacy of international education in terms of 'immersion' and responsibilisation (Kristensen, 2001).

When this programme began in 1992 the student cohort was made up of equal numbers of students from Denmark and the UK. The practice opportunities were varied and the students were able to spend the last term comparing and contrasting their different placement opportunities. This led McNay (1994) to suggest that placements were one of the most succesful aspects of the programme. As she commented, 'Many students from both the UK and Denmark have felt the role of the foreign student offers opportunities to make mistakes or ask basic questions with a certain degree of security' (p. 17).

Horncastle and Brobeck (1995) looked at the practice experience from the position of the practice supervisor. They noted how the Danish practice teachers rated highly the usefulness of the practice experience. They drew attention to the comment of one practitioner that, 'cross cultural experience is nearly always useful. It is wonderful that students can see social work through different eyes, to give more insights and perspectives' (p. 50). They also cite one UK placement where the practice supervisor commented on how one student was 'a different person afterwards' (p. 50). However, they identified two major problems with arranging such placements – language competency and lack of knowledge of the different welfare systems in place in each country.

In the recent operation of the programme (2000–2004), the issue of language competency has been eased by the absence of UK students from the programme, given that the Danish and other Scandinavian students are highly competent in English (enabling appropriate communication with users or workers on placement). However, this problem may recur because the programme is seeking validation at post-qualifiying level, which may attract a new cohort of UK students. In this event, access to Portsmouth University's substantial language programme prior to placement may alleviate potential problems. Certainly, students accessing a European option within the new social work degree at Portsmouth will be expected to prepare thoroughly (including linguistically) for any placement that they may undertake outside the UK.

The issue about students lacking knowledge of the different welfare traditions has been systematically tackled within the programmme. The units outlined above are comparative in all respects. The students undertake additional units on European social work and focus on issues of comparative methodology in the research module. By the time they submit their dissertations they should have developed an ability to critically analyse a comprehensive range of material.

It would therefore appear that the students can become 'immersed' in the environments in which they are placed. They become very involved with the population of the country in the locality where they are placed and often engage in cultural and social activities while in the host country (for example, through joining athletics, swimming or climbing clubs; or playing music in local bars). The practice settings in which they are placed also provide an opportunity for them to demonstrate competence as autonomous practitioners. Initially it was thought that placements should be primarily observational. It is now accepted that the students already have experience of placements on their own programmes and often work part time in quite complex welfare environmments. Placements have therefore become more challenging and students have been tested in stressful and demanding placements, such as in advocacy projects, mental health units, projects working with single homeless people or women escaping violence, and in Youth Offending Teams. This may involve them undertaking work that carries some statutory responsibilities including attending court, representing service users at tribunals, or dealing with emotionally scarred young people. Clearly they attain the degree of 'responsibilisation' mentioned by Kristensen.

However, a supplementary issue has arisen despite the attempts to promote pedagogy as an approach in the UK. This relates to the students' experience not so much of the placement or of the policy framework underpinning it. Although they may be unfamilair with these issues early on, they develop quite sophisticated understandings of these issues as the placement progresses. This refers instead to what Lorenz calls the dialectics of care and control (Lorenz, 2002). Drawing on pedagogical traditions, Lorenz suggests that, 'In all social interventions boundaries have to be negotiated rather than assumed, and these boundaries, as we know from pedagogical contexts, have to be legitimated not with the power we bring to bear in defining them for others but by elaborating a shared meaning of boundaries with all participants' (Lorenz, 2002, p. 13).

This echoes the idea of the common third mentioned above and points to a real issue for international, particularly Danish, students experiencing the UK practice environment. The participative and empowering strategies, central to the common third (and project-based work), have become marginalised within UK social work, particularly statutory social work, where, partly as the legacy of numerous enquiries and reports, British social workers have become risk averse or at the very least concerned with the management of risk. As Beck suggests, 'To the same degree as sensitivity to risk grows in the public, a political need for minimization research arises' (Beck, 1992, p. 226). Such an approach can lead to what Buckley, writing about the Irish child protection system, suggests is 'a discourse that is essentially bureaucratic, defined by management and prescription without considerations of the imperfections, organic weaknesses or uncertainties of 'real life" (Buckley, 2003).

International students on the programme have often commented on such scenarios. One student, when placed in a small residential unit for young people, could not believe that the police were called for a minor disturbance when in her experience such a situation would have been resolved by discussion and negotiation if it had occurred in Denmark. Others have commented on the bureaucratic nature of the care management process or of the way risk assessment has become such a major factor in all interventions but particularly those with young people. At the same time, students frequently comment on the importance of recognising the different needs of different groups of service users and see this as a strength of the UK approach.

Conclusion

The Portsmouth–Frobel Seminariet BA ESW degree is currently unique in providing a full-time programme of study for undergraduate students from a range of European countries. A number of universities provide European options in year 3 for students studying social work (for example, University College Cork, Ireland, as well as in the UK). This course is different in that students study a joint curriculum, which draws on academic traditions from the UK and other European countries and which is jointly delivered by staff from a number of institutions. For instance, in addition to the input from Frobel and Portsmouth, a colleague from Freiburg (Germany) provides teaching on intercultural communication during the Danish part of the course.

It is suggested that substantial learning about the work of social professionals can be derived from collaborations of the kind discussed above. In-depth understanding of the importance of different histories, social policies and value systems can help us meet the needs of undergraduate students who are seeking to expand their horizons beyond their country of origin.

Notes

1   However, the introduction of student loans and the need to pay tuition fees seriously depleted the number of UK students attending the programme subsequently. It is too soon to say whether changes in qualifying course length and the introduction of bursaries from 2004 will lead to an increase in take-up by UK students.

2   Denmark was chosen as a partner at least partly because many Danish students are competent in the English language and because it would provide an opportunity for UK students, who traditionally do not have such a language facility, to study in another country (McNay, 1994).

3   For example, the Skovtofke Seminarium had a total student number of 350, the University of Portsmouth has 20,000 students. The Frobel Seminariet is bigger but still has only about 1,000 students.

4   Social ardgivers in Denmark perform some of the statutory roles performed by social workers in the UK combined with the role of administration within the social benefits system (Harder, 1997).

5   These sections draws on discussions and correspondence with colleagues in Denmark (particularly Christian Aabro and Karen Prins, lecturers at Frobel Seminariet), discussions with students and particularly the recent dissertation by Laika Borghill (2004), which specifically addressed the concept of the 'common third'.

Chapter 7

Post graduate provision in Europe

Sue Lawrence

Introduction

European Union (EU) education policy has been central in paving the way for facilitating developments that might lead to harmonisation in higher education and cultural integration. It is envisaged that the European Higher Education Area (EHEA), which the EU aims to establish by 2010, will facilitate and encourage mobility and transferability for all staff and students engaged in undergraduate and postgraduate study as well as for those engaged in research (discussed in Chapters 2 and 4). A range of pan-European educational activities has flowed from these policies, giving rise to both greater acknowledgement of differences in systems and practices, and the development of new European paradigms.

The location of education and training for social professionals in Europe is mainly in the tertiary sector: in post-secondary vocational polytechnics or other 'applied' higher education institutions, for example, Hogeschoolen in the Netherlands, *Fachhochschulen* in Germany and Hojskolen in Denmark; and mainly, although not exclusively, in universities, for example in the UK, Ireland and Finland (see Chapter 3). From 1987 to 1995 when Inter-university Co-operation Programmes (ICPs) were being formed under the first Erasmus programme, those non-university institutions responsible for social work professional education were not able to deliver programmes beyond Bachelor degree level. The universities in those countries tended to be reserved for the more traditional academic disciplines, social work being considered an applied or vocational subject area. If students wanted to go on to study at postgraduate level in their own country, they would have to look to an 'academic discipline' (for example, law, psychology or sociology), and their qualification in the social professions would not always guarantee meeting postgraduate entrance criteria.

In this context, some of the newly formed Erasmus ICP networks decided to pool their growing knowledge of the study of social work in Europe and jointly develop Masters programmes facilitated by curriculum development funding from the Erasmus scheme. It was envisaged that these programmes would embrace a European, comparative or international dimension in an attempt to satisfy students wanting to study beyond their basic national professional qualification. Institutions without the authority to validate at postgraduate level often looked to network partners with such competence, usually ones where social work education was located in the university sector. In this way, collaborative postgraduate programmes were developed that did not follow a particular pattern or model, but which arose from the combination of the partners and their growing interest, experience, expertise and enthusiasm for social work at a European level.

The outcome for social professionals has been a variety of programmes that have 'European' in their title, or as a major component of the curriculum, a trend that has continued through the Socrates scheme since 1996. While there is no agreed definition of the content of this 'European dimension', various developments in curricula for the social professions took place that have been grouped into three main types (Lorenz, 1998, p. 140):

● The 'Europeanisation' of existing courses by including some additional comparative material.
● The creation of new, self-contained 'European' modules to add to an existing programme.
● The creation of whole new courses with a 'European' focus, mainly at postgraduate or post-qualifying level.

It is the last category, the area of 'European' education for social professionals at postgraduate and/or post-qualifying level that is the focus of this chapter. The range of postgraduate study and research that has contributed to continuing professional development in 'European social work' includes Masters programmes; doctoral study and research degrees; and research and scholarly activity. For those involved in the delivery of postgraduate European programmes in the early 1990s, finding published sources that addressed the themes and issues to be addressed in European social work courses was a challenge. However, a new range of publications came on stream, stimulating, supporting and reflecting the course developments taking place, including two journals, *Social Work in Europe* (1994–2003) and the *European Journal of Social Work* (1998–present and since 2004 incorporating *Social Work in Europe*). There has also been an increase in relevant books published in the UK, varying from issue-based and thematic texts (Cannan et al., 1992; Lorenz, 1994) through comparative texts (such as Adams et al., 2000) to books focusing on specific client groups, such as children (Pringle, 1998) or elders (Hugman, 1994). Additionally, edited books arising from the conferences and seminars initiated by particular networks, including ECSPRESS (the thematic network of the social professions), were published particularly in Germany, utilising both the German and English languages and sometimes others (see for instance, Seibel and Lorenz, 1998; Chytil and Seibel, 1999; Chytil et al., 2000).

Therefore there is now a wealth of European, international and/or comparative texts available on relevant subjects that, taken together with websites and grey literature from the European Commission (EC) and other European bodies (including the voluntary sector), can sometimes result in a sense of information overload for staff and students alike. Advanced skills in information management are now a prerequisite for successful study at postgraduate level for European social professionals.

Issues in developing European postgraduate provision: The MACESS example

As well as Erasmus and Socrates, other EU programmes, such as Tempus, Leonardo and the European Social Fund have contributed to the development of postgraduate initiatives. In some cases these projects resulted from and expanded programmes that were already established, and in others, new partnerships came together and developed new programmes or courses. To illustrate the diversity of European postgraduate provision in this field, examples of a range of programmes are presented below, beginning with a detailed profile of the Maastricht-based MA Comparative European Social Studies (MACESS), as one of the first Erasmus-funded postgraduate European programmes for the social professions.

MACESS was the product of an Erasmus Network, which began in 1991 with six cooperating institutions from Belgium, France, Germany, the UK and the

Netherlands. The Network was coordinated by the Hogeschool Maastricht (subsequently Zuyd) (the Netherlands), which successfully applied to Erasmus in 1993 for funding for a curriculum development project for a European Masters degree programme for social professionals. The Dutch education system at that time had sufficient resources and flexibility for the development and delivery of the programme and the geographical location of Maastricht and its symbolic significance as being the site of the 1992 Treaty made it an obvious and appropriate choice for the course base. The University of North London (subsequently London Metropolitan University) in the UK was chosen from within the network to validate the programme as it offered a clear, comprehensive and developmental system of validation, quality assurance and review.

The programme, which lasts for one calendar year (three terms), was developed and successfully validated in June 1994 and in September 1994 it received its first intake of 19 full-time students. The original programme was changed to its current format two years later, based on feedback from students, lecturers and the external examiner, and the programme was developed further to reflect important social and political issues and student interests. The result of this development was to designate four of the modules plus the dissertation as 'core' modules and to have five optional modules (see Table 7.1), from which students have to choose two (Lawrence and Reverda, 1998).

Table 7.1 Core and option modules on MACESS

Core modules	Option modules

European institutions and policy
Comparative social policy
Comparative social research
Social professional practice in
  Europe
Dissertation
	European network development
	Managing change in a European
	  context
	Marginalisation and social exclusion
	Political philosophy and European
	  welfare
	European welfare law

Experience on the MACESS programme has resulted in the identification of a number of issues, which have relevance to similar developments.

Institutional impact and arrangements

Both Hogeschool Zuyd (created 1 September 2001) and London Metropolitan University (created 1 August 2002) have been the subject of higher education mergers. The institutional fallout of such processes is always considerable for those involved and the MACESS management task in both instances was to provide a stable environment through effective liaison and interpretation of any new policies resulting from both mergers. The position of the programme slightly 'outside' the 'normal frameworks' of both institutions in some cases proved useful in shielding the programme from direct impact, but in other situations it had the opposite effect in terms of being a 'special case' needing additional consideration.

The Hogeschool Zuyd initially had to invest heavily in expanding its library stock to include a whole range of relevant texts and journals in English for a postgraduate programme for the social professions. This investment continued with a substantial annual budget. Dedicated networked computers for the MACESS students were also provided in a classroom used solely for the programme. Personnel at every level of the Hogeschool Zuyd had to accommodate the influx of MACESS lecturers and students, operating at a different academic level, in foreign languages and representing many different cultures and backgrounds.

Issues relating to regulations and quality assurance have posed some interesting challenges to standard academic regulations. Although the MACESS programme operates under London Metropolitan University regulations, aspects of Dutch law and regulations governing some procedures require delicate interpretation and implementation so as not to disadvantage students, who could easily fall through the gap between those two systems. Examinations are such an example, where the Hogeschool Zuyd dictates policy for the conduct of exams, procedures for extenuation and has a policy of automatic 're-sits' for every student each year. Operating a system that is subject to two sets of rules is complex and the management task here has been to ensure that both sets of regulations work in harmony, allowing the dominant regulations precedence in each instance. This complexity is managed by ensuring that all contact with the host institution is made through the course director (London), who has been able to negotiate the sensitive application of university rules with the registry.

Coordination and network development

The MACESS Network developed from the Erasmus ICP network described above and has expanded to include 35 institutions including the EC and the Council of Europe (CoE) (see www.macess.nl for details). It has been categorised as an example of an 'expansive network' and is representative of the variety of social professional education and training awards in Europe (in social work, social pedagogy, youth and community work, social cultural work, and social education) (Seibel and Lorenz, 1998, p. 136). The Network has proved to be a central feature of the MACESS programme, providing most of the guest lecturers and recruiting most of its students each year. The Network currently meets once a year to organise staff and student recruitment and exchange and to discuss any issues relevant to both the programme and social professional practice. Network meetings are scheduled to coincide with any conferences or seminars organised by European or international social professional bodies (for example, the European Association of Schools of Social Work [EASSW], International Association of Schools of Social Work [IASSW], and the Formation d'Educateurs Sociaux Europeens [FESET, European Social Educators Training) to facilitate attendance.

To ensure coherence within the programme and to encourage appropriate development within each module, twice-yearly course team meetings are held to review and evaluate input, output and student feedback. Module convenors give a report to the course team based on this information, which, coupled with external examiner and assessment board reports, provide vital information for the improvement and updating of the programme and contribute to the data required for quality assurance purposes. In addition to this, any issues or developments arising in discrete subject areas or more generally, provide themes for wider discussion and staff development.

Assessment processes

As indicated in Chapter 6, different institutions have individual approaches to assessment, with regions or countries having different practices and traditions in this area. For the MACESS students, with their 10 convenors, 35 markers, and moderators from as many as 23 different countries there is potential for misunderstanding and conflict. Various strategies have been put into place in an attempt to develop an assessment framework, which addresses 'European' issues arising from the diverse nature of the programme and its participants. London Metropolitan University regulations require all postgraduate assignments to be double marked. Each module convenor appoints, where possible, two markers who represent different regions or traditions. This is the case also for the dissertation, but here, the dissertation supervisor can represent any one of the 23 countries linked to MACESS and that person, who may never visit Maastricht, only has one piece of work to mark. The second marker is either from London or Maastricht, to ensure that the two markers are from different regions. Here, however, there has sometimes been wide variation in marks given, resulting from different traditions and expectations of postgraduate dissertations in different institutions and countries. To address this issue, an experienced external moderator has been appointed, with knowledge of the course and different educational traditions, for third marking. In addition, in line with London Metropolitan University requirements, a sample of all assessed work is sent to the external examiner, appointed by the university to ensure that consistent and appropriate standards of marking are applied. Any particular issues are raised at the assessment board, held annually, chaired by a senior manager from London Metropolitan University and attended by the course directors, module convenors and the external examiner to assure academic standards and fair play within the context of such diversity.

Student funding, entry and outcomes

The unequal geographical distribution of entrants to the MACESS course can be closely linked to the impact of diverse funding streams in different countries and through some institutions. The course fee for EU citizens was €2340 for the full-time programme in 2004, with living expenses additional to this amount. Some students from partner institutions in the MACESS Network are entitled to Socrates student funding at postgraduate level, but this pays only a proportion of the overall costs of fees and living expenses. Between 1995 and 1998 a Tempus project enabled students from Hungary to join the course, fully funded. However, since that time, very few Hungarian students have been able to afford to join the programme (a situation that may change with the admission of Hungary to the EU). Three students from Croatia were fully funded by the Croatian government to study on the MACESS programme (one each over successive years).

Some countries (for example, Denmark, Finland and Norway) have provided state grants to students to cover the cost of postgraduate education, while other students have received sabbatical grants from employers. In some countries (for example, Belgium, the Netherlands and Germany) students begin their social professional education at 18 years of age and some therefore still enjoy financial support from their parents when they join the MACESS programme in their early twenties. All of the countries in the above categories have therefore been well represented. Very few students (seven in all) from the UK have participated, partly due to the likely older age at which students qualify in social work or youth and community work, making it more likely that domestic commitments and student debt discourage further study and/or study away from home. The course team continue to seek funding opportunities for students through bursaries and scholarships. See Table 7.2 for data on MACESS students' country of origin.

Table 7.2 Country of origin of MACESS students (n=238)

Country of origin	Number	Country of origin	Number
Albania	1	Italy	4
Austria	6	The Netherlands	35
Belgium	25	Northern Ireland	1
Bulgaria	1	Norway	29
Croatia	3	Poland	2
Denmark	19	Portugal	2
Finland	9	Rumania	1
France	5	Spain	10
Germany	48	Sweden	2
Greece	3	Switzerland	2
Hungary	15	Turkey	1
Iceland	1	Uganda	1
Ireland	3	UK	7

MACESS has proven to be a robust programme over a 10-year period, recruiting viable numbers of students and responding to developments in specific subject areas and student interests, by drawing guest lecturers and dissertation supervisors from a diverse range of countries within and beyond the EU (see Table 7.3).

Table 7.3 MACESS course statistics

Year	Students	Graduates	Convenors	Guest lecturers	Dissertation supervisors
1994/95	19	19	7	15	19
1995/96	21	20	7	21	21
1996/97	30	28	10	48	30
1997/98	28	18	10	54	29
1998/99	23	25	10	49	23
1999/2000	23	18	10	51	26
2000/01	23	15	10	47	16
2001/02	29 (1pt)	22	10	50	28
2002/03	23(3pt)	21	10	49	20
2003/04	25 (4pt)	19	10	45	24

Note: pt=part-time students

In the first 10 years of the programme, 205 people graduated from the programme and have been employed in a very wide variety of positions at European, national, regional and local level. The graduates seeking employment in the social professions reflect their status on entry to the MACESS programme. Newly qualified and younger people take more junior social work posts, whereas graduates who were senior practitioners or managers often use the qualification to advance their careers. Some graduates seek employment outside of the social professions, using their qualification to demonstrate more general or transferable knowledge and skills. A further group of MACESS graduates have secured positions in European or international organisations, such as the CoE, the EC and various international non-governmental organisations or charities (personal communications).

Recognition and validation

As an English Master of Arts (MA) degree, MACESS is recognised within the UK, with appropriate standing in an international context. For some MACESS graduates this has been sufficient when presenting the award during an application for employment, or for other academic courses. Some students, however, have encountered difficulties in gaining recognition for their qualification where uncertainty about equivalence to national qualifications has posed problems. A pragmatic approach has therefore been taken with regard to the status of the award, with any requests for information by students, institutions or national validating bodies being appropriately answered. In addition, MACESS has had formal recognition in Germany since 1999, and Croatia since 2002, which has been helpful for students wanting to go on to other academic programmes in those countries. However, the lack of a common process for recognition of postgraduate awards in Europe has been acknowledged from the inception of the MACESS programme and students have been made aware of the nature and limitations of the award. The establishment of a postgraduate framework under the Bologna agreement will go some way to addressing this issue (Lawrence and Reverda, 2000).

Other examples and models of European postgraduate provision

The MSc in European Social Work based initially in Canterbury (UK) is a very recent example of a Socrates-funded curriculum development programme drawing on the European Social Fund for student financial support. It aims to provide a unified programme operating across European higher educational institutions leading to a common award. Staff at Canterbury Christ Church University College (UK) led development of the programme, and other partners include the University of Salford (UK), Catholic University of Eichstatt (Germany), University of Ostrava (Czechoslovakia), University of Kuopio (Finland), Catholic University of Lille (France), University of Utrecht (the Netherlands), University of Trento (Italy), University of Calabria (Italy), Ramon Lull University, Barcelona (Spain), University of Tartu (Estonia). The four core modules on the programme are: The Construction of Social Work in Europe; The Practice of Social Work in Europe; The Management of Social Work in Europe; and Comparative Research in European Social Work. There are also thematic options, some of which require study in a partner institution or at international seminars, and finally there is a research project leading to a dissertation. The entry requirements to the programme are a social work qualification, or a degree in a relevant subject plus a minimum of two years' experience in a social care setting. The programme will normally be taken on a part-time basis, or if full time, access to practice is required. The first student intake was in the academic session 2003–04 (Adams and Shardlow, 2002).

The Alice Salomon Fachhochschulen in Berlin is home to another example of postgraduate provision: a Master of Social Work in 'Intercultural Work and Conflict Management'. This is a programme developed by a single institution for an international market, with funding from the German government. The first intake was in the 2000–01 session. For the first two years the Deutscher Akademischer Austauschdienst (DAA) – the German Academic Exchange Service – financially supported students via scholarships. It is a three-term programme for graduates of social work with a national professional qualification. It comprises internet courses of three months duration in the first and third terms, with taught classes in Berlin of six weeks duration also during these terms. There is a four-month placement in the second term. The course is taught in English in the first term and in German in the third term. Language support is available to all participating students. Recruitment was buoyant in the first two years, but has been lower since the gradual reduction of financial support from the DAA.

An academic project of a very different kind was initiated in Romania in the form of a qualifying social work training programme at postgraduate level that used Tempus-Phare grant funding. Academic, government and agency partners from four different countries were involved in the project – Romania, Northern Ireland, the Republic of Ireland and The Netherlands. Partners comprised the University of Transylvania; the Romanian government and non-governmental organisations in the Brasov area; the University of Ulster; Eastern Health and Social Services Board (Northern Ireland); the Northern Ireland Association for Mental Health; the Western Health and Social Services Board (Northern Ireland); Ulster Community and Hospital Trust (Northern Ireland); Trinity College Dublin (Ireland); and Nijmegen Instituut in the Netherlands. The aim was to develop a two-year part-time Postgraduate Diploma in Social Work to train much-needed social workers in the newly independent country of Romania. Planning began in 1996, but the first Tempus application for an undergraduate programme did not meet with success, as it did not satisfy all Tempus requirements. The second application was successful, as a two-year postgraduate programme was submitted with the addition of a health dimension to the original social work and social care curriculum. Five Romanian practice teachers were trained within the Tempus project to provide placements during the students' first year. The second-year placements were in one of the three EU countries of the Tempus project partnership. There were 22 students in the first cohort in 1998, of which 19 graduated in November 2000. All were Honours graduates, 11 having been seconded by Brasov County Department of Child Protection, following the Romanian government target of reducing the number of children in orphanages. The strategic priorities in 1999 were to achieve Postgraduate Diploma academic status in Romania; professional accreditation in Romania; and integration into European Credit Transfer System (ECTS) (Bamford et al., 2000).

An article by Bamford and Ross (2003) identified various significant matters arising from the programme, including:

● the accreditation of the award in Romania in 2000;
● a fund set up to support payment of course fees because of student poverty;
● time commitments given by Western European partners to ensure post-Tempus sustainability;
● the role of the new graduates on the programme as practice teachers and lecturers;
● the difficulty of assessing practice in the context of developing services;
● preparing practice teachers by having them undertake programmes in the three participating Western European countries and providing ongoing support to them;
● the importance of strategic networking, negotiation and collaboration in developing partnerships in Romania between teachers on the programme and local social care agencies;

- the rigidity of Tempus rules and deadlines that were sometimes obstructive to the project; and
- the importance of disseminating the outcome of the project to share the learning to a wider audience, both in Romania and internationally.

Spin-offs included the support of social care projects in Romania by Western European partners; and the verification of the Romanian award by the General Social Care Council in the UK (Bamford and Ross, 2003).

Finally, another alternative model of a postgraduate European social work programme is afforded by a UK-based course that locates national and European developments in an international context. The MA in International Social Work at the University of East London owes its origins to experience at undergraduate level of active participation in an Erasmus network as well as to recognition of the fact that, for many students in a multicultural part of London, European countries were not a preferred destination for further learning. Initial development of the MA in International Social Work was carried out with partners from Austria, Germany, Greece (supported by a Socrates Curriculum Development grant, 1998–2000) and also Switzerland.

The programme was validated by the University of East London in summer 2000 as an MA in International Social Work with Community Development Studies, and an additional pathway – International Social Work with Refugee Studies – was added in 2001. The original intention was for the course to be offered by all five partners, with particular institutions hosting modules that reflected their expertise. However, this proved difficult in the early stages for a variety of reasons (including changes in national higher education policies and institutional arrangements in partner institutions) and provision is currently on offer only in London. The original network partners retain some contact, and support the programme through advertising and passing on enquiries, but to some extent the programme has since developed on a different basis than one reliant on formal partnerships (see below).

The small size of the network promoting the development (together with other factors) perhaps partly accounted for an initially small intake (from September 2000), although numbers increased to an annual intake of around 20 by the third and fourth years of operation. Similarly, the numbers graduating to date have been relatively small (26 by 2004), related partly to the fact that some students choose to take the course part time, extending their studies beyond the three terms that constitute the normal full-time length.

Recruitment has presented some interesting dilemmas since applications come (literally it seems) from all over the world (many by e-mail). Decisions about eligibility are made on the basis of a written application, together with evidence of awards, linguistic competence (if necessary) and references. In addition, communication sometimes takes place by telephone or e-mail. Many applicants see the course as an opportunity to gain a 'professional' qualification in social work, despite publicity stating that a social work qualification (or a nationally recognised equivalent) is normally a pre-requisite for selection. However, judgements have to be made about when applicants are unlikely to have had opportunities to gain such a qualification but have appropriate experience as well as relevant academic awards. Additionally, it seems likely that the fact that, to date, the programme has not sought recognition within the British framework for post-qualifying professional awards may have discouraged some local social workers from applying.

However, students have been recruited from a wide range of countries (sometimes direct from their country of origin and sometimes from those who have arrived in the UK or another EU country relatively recently) as follows: Australia, Bangladesh, Bosnia Herzgovina (via Belgium), Canada, Ethiopia (via Sweden), Germany, Ghana (via the UK), Greece, India, Kosova (via the UK), the Netherlands, Nigeria, Pakistan, Senegal, Sierra Leone (via the UK), Somalia (via the UK), South Africa, Spain, Uganda, the UK, the US and Zimbabwe (via the UK). Numerically, students qualifying to pay home or EU fees outnumber 'overseas' students, but overall, the annual intakes comprise a rich mix of students with different cultural, ethnic, linguistic, national and religious backgrounds, constituting an important element in the learning environment. Students tend to divide fairly evenly between those following the respective pathways ('with Community Development Studies' or 'with Refugee Studies').

All students take core units in *International Social Work* and *Researching and Learning* (30 credits each), as well as a *Dissertation* unit (60 credits), and the two options taken (as well as the topic for the dissertation) reflect the chosen pathway/intended award. Institutional changes, in the form of modularisation of all postgraduate courses in 2004, have strengthened existing working relationships with other Masters programmes, such as Refugee Studies, Voluntary Sector Studies, and International Law, from which international social work students can choose options.

As indicated above, a particular aspect of the course has been the move away from formal partnerships, which, while they may advantage some students financially, could 'lock them in' to particular destinations for their project work

– although, given the recruitment patterns of the course and the coming on stream of the Erasmus Mundus programme (see later) it may be timely to review this position. However, to date, the programme has been developed on the principle that students are free to choose the destination for their project work (which forms the basis of the Dissertation unit), as well as the focus. This entails staff in the home institution taking responsibility for the supervision of such students (usually carried out via e-mail while the students are away), following a period of regular project group meetings in the preparatory phase. The establishment of close working relations and interest in other students' research plans, through discussion in the project groups, has often meant that peer support continues to be an important element at the stage when students are dispersed doing their individual projects – although some have proved very resourceful in also linking into local resource and support networks in their project destinations.

As with other programmes that bring together students from different cultural and educational traditions, one of the main issues identified in the early stages related to marking standards and conventions, including some students' concerns about marks in the 50s and 60s (in a scheme where the pass mark is 50, and average marks of 65% or 75% result in an award with a merit or distinction, respectively). The staff team regularly have to explain UK social science conventions in which marks in the 70s or higher are relatively rare, those in the 60s can be seen as good and those in the 50s quite acceptable, relative to other countries where a much wider range of marks would be in evidence. There are also issues around written English where English is not the student's mother tongue, and occasionally this has shaded into plagiarism where students have failed to put text into their own words, sometimes for linguistic reasons but also related to concerns about questioning or altering the words of authors (who are seen as experts).

In general, the issue of recognition has not yet been a problem, although in one country (where social work is not offered at university level) a student's application for a university PhD programme was not accepted. As indicated, most students already hold country-specific professional qualifications and the trend, to date, has been for many students to return to a home country or alternatively to aim for work in an international organisation. The latter may require them to get additional relevant experience first so some stay in London initially and get jobs through employment agencies (see also Chapter 8).

A summary of the different models of the postgraduate European programmes is presented in Table 7.4 below.

Table 7.4 Key features of European postgraduate programmes

Course title	Host institution	Validated by	First intake	Development funding source	Student funding	Network size	Countries involved
MA Comparative European Social Studies	Hogeschool Zuyd, NL	London Metropolitan University, UK	1994	Erasmus Curriculum Development Grant	Socrates Mobility Grants (subject to eligibility)	40	24
MSc European Social Work	Canterbury Christchurch University College, UK	Canterbury Christchurch University College, UK	2003	Socrates Curriculum Development Grant	European Social Fund (UK students)	11	9
MA in Social Work 'Intercultural Work and Conflict Management'	Alice Salomon Fachhochschule, D	Alice Salomon Fachhochschule, D	2000	German government	Deutscher Akademischer Austauschdienst (for first two years only)	N/K	N/K
Postgraduate Diploma in Social Work	University of Transylvania	University of Transylvania	1998	Tempus	Brasov County Department of Child Protection; Tempus funding; Trust Fund	9+	4
MA in International Social Work	University of East London	University of East London	2000	Socrates Curriculum Development Grant	Socrates Mobility Grants (first three years only)	5	5

New expectations and opportunities

As previous chapters have indicated, significant developments are occurring in higher education and these are impacting on postgraduate provision for social work professionals in a number of ways, some of which are discussed below.

Research-minded practitioners

The students on European or international postgraduate courses produce a variety of cross-national or comparative dissertations or country-specific case studies set in a wider European or international context. These studies have covered many topics and have yielded a rich source of information in different forms and of varying standards.

It is evident that such studies contribute to the knowledge base of the profession and that many research-minded practitioners with the benefit of European and/or international perspectives are graduating from such programmes. However, there are few discernable commonalities between such student dissertations, other than that the topics are all connected in some way to social professional concerns and have a European or international dimension. In relation to the MACESS dissertations, an attempt to examine the complexity of comparative research as a methodology for exploring social work has been made, as a contribution to developing European perspectives on social policy and social work theory and practice. The dissertations can usually be identified as being on topics related to policy, topics related to practice and those that are a combination of both policy and practice. The task of trying to categorise these studies is made more difficult by the different theoretical perspectives from which the students approach 'social work' and 'social research'.

On the basis of this analysis, an epistemological framework of scientific approaches to knowledge development and ways of knowing has been suggested, which range from modern to post-modern, from the legislator to the interpreter. This also represents a paradigm shift as research models and methods are deconstructed and reconstructed in the move from 'traditional' scientific approaches (modern) to 'new' alternative or naturalistic paradigms (post-modern). The other factor to be considered is the ontology of the 'social' as a way of being a social worker and/or a social researcher. The axis between these two factors reflects the professional identification that can be ascertained in the way that students consider themselves as social workers or as researchers within the context of social research and whether they see the research as a 'change agent' in itself. In this sense, every study has both content and context and both social work and research are reflections of the students' different starting points. The model offered suggests that post-modernity demands a re-appraisal of 'professional identity' and provides a vehicle for the exploration of what the future may be for social work (Richardson and Lawrence, 2005).

Turning to the possibility of people in the social professions choosing to engage in further postgraduate study through research at doctoral level, as already indicated (Chapter 4) the possibility to do this in the subject area of social work (or similar) – relative to through more conventional disciplines (such as sociology or psychology) – varies by country. In the late 1990s, a French school, Ecole Supérieure de Travail Social (ETSUP), received funding from the European Social Fund to investigate, with partners, the opportunities for – and output of – doctoral work in and about social work (broadly defined). This proved to be a more difficult task than might have originally been envisaged, not least related to defining the scope of social work as an area of study at this level. The task was made more complex because of the difficulties and subtleties of intercultural communication between the partners from a range of European countries in attempting to find equivalence in scientific and institutional terms, concepts and procedures. An early finding was that few countries had recognised social work doctoral programmes in place and that fewer still had national registers or data about doctorates completed in the broad social professional field.

The research therefore took the form of in-depth enquiries into the form of 11 doctoral programmes in the partner countries – Belgium, England, Finland, Germany, Hungary, Ireland, Italy, Poland, Portugal, Sweden and Switzerland. This approach revealed significant variation in programmes and these seemed to be institutionally specific, providing little indication of clear national models (Laot, 2000). One such example concerns the development of 'professional doctorates'. The case studied in the UK (University of East Anglia) provided a very different model from conventional PhDs, although it is a format (including some taught elements and employment-related course work as well as specific research projects) that may well be gaining in popularity and be particularly well suited to the needs and interests of social workers and related professionals (whether involved in direct practice or management of services). Interestingly, so far this form of PhD (already developed in the fields of education, psychology and management) is only available to social professionals in the UK and some Nordic countries; and, in general, it is likely that students will need to enrol in programmes of related disciplines (rather than social work) the further south one goes in Europe (Lyons, 2003). As indicated in Chapter 4, this project laid an important basis for a subsequent project (Centre Européen de Ressources pour la Recherche en Travail Social – CERTS, also funded by the European Social Fund) to establish a European database of doctoral and comparable research studies, which could be used as a source of information about topics selected and methodology employed by social workers, as well as a resource for people wanting to establish networks around common concerns.

E-learning and distance learning

Courses established in the early 1990s relied entirely on face-to-face teaching, using the diverse student group as a vehicle for learning. It is difficult to imagine now, but at that time, the use of computers, even for simple word processing, was by no means widespread across Europe. As technology has developed, examples have increased where learning technology has been used and developed to support teaching within courses. The students coming to such courses today are increasingly computer literate and many have very advanced skills in the area of information retrieval and management. The student group, therefore, expects courses to utilise current information technologies in their teaching and learning strategies. The use of the internet as a resource for information is as commonly used on postgraduate European courses as elsewhere in higher education. E-learning platforms are also beginning to be considered in many programmes and are already in use on some (for example on the MACESS programme).

Distance learning has not been taken up readily as a solution for engaging a scattered European student population. The importance of a real rather than virtual lecturer and the learning to be gained within a pan-European or international group of students within an area of study – the human services – which by definition uses face-to-face contact as a tool of the trade, cannot be underestimated. However, examples of the utilisation of distance-learning materials used in conjunction with intensive taught elements of courses are now in evidence, for example on the programme based at Alice Salomon Fachhochschulen.

The impact of the Bologna Process

As part of the Bologna Process to harmonise degree structures and the introduction of compatible qualifications at the undergraduate and postgraduate level across Europe, the European Universities Association

(EUA) coordinated a one-year Joint European Masters Project in 2002-03, partly funded under Socrates. The study aimed to examine the current European provision of Joint European Masters degrees and to disseminate examples of good practice, while at the same time, highlighting the experience gained by the collaborative networks to move from 'good practice' to 'best practice'. The project further aimed to improve the quality of mobility, establish the optimal conditions for the running of cooperative programmes at Masters level and to feed results into the subsequent conferences in Graz and Berlin in Germany in 2003, to assist the Bologna Process.

At a programme level, the European Universities Association (EUA, 2002) stipulated the following conditions in its call for applications for the Joint European Masters Project and in doing so, laid down some guidelines for what it considered to be 'Joint European Masters' prerequisites:

● *Partnership*: between at least three universities in three different countries.
● *Mobility*: existence of both student and staff mobility between the institutions participating in the programme.
● *Language*: institutions should have a clearly identifiable language policy. For example, this could include language training or other induction courses, if programmes are taught in a language other than that of the host institution.
● *Course integration*: partners should demonstrate that thought has been given to arrangements made for either delivering curricula developed jointly, or to ensuring that full recognition is given to course units developed and delivered separately by the different partners in the Consortium.
● *Diploma or degree awarded*: based on the legislation in force in the partner countries involved, the Consortium should be able to define clearly the nature and form of the final diploma/s delivered, for example, as one diploma endorsed by all universities involved or as two or several separate degree certificates.
● *Quality assurance*: transparent procedures should be agreed and in place from the beginning, such as jointly agreed criteria for admission and examination.

The EUA had 60 applications from networks running European Masters courses, and from those, 11 networks (involving 73 European universities or colleges of higher education) were chosen to participate. MACESS was selected as the Joint European Masters for the social professions – the other

10 networks covered a very diverse subject range, including European construction engineering and international health and tropical medicine.

Each network participated in a commonly developed action research project to identify and document the factors for successful cooperation. This information was then analysed and informed a report highlighting three headline issues: curriculum integration and sustainability, student experience and mobility, and quality assurance and recognition. These topics formed the framework for discussion at a seminar of participating networks in Bilbao in April 2003. A final evaluation report recommended how the project could inform issues on a wider European level, having identified the following as requiring further action to facilitate current and future Joint European Masters programmes (EUA, 2003):

- amending national legislation to enable higher education institutions across Europe to award joint degrees;
- developing appropriate quality assurance and recognition mechanisms for such programmes, hopefully with a 'European' label;
- anchoring joint programmes firmly within institutional structures;
- reducing tuition fee and cost-of-living imbalances for mobile students across Europe;
- targeting financial support to students with the greatest financial needs;
- securing stable financing for the coherent development of programmes;
- maximising potential to develop research cooperation;
- using existing tools such as ECTS and the Diploma Supplement effectively.

While the recommendations of the Joint Masters Project have immediate significance for European postgraduate programmes, the more general developments arising from the Bologna Process are also having an impact. The Bologna formulation of the preferred pattern of higher education into the '3-5-8' model (three years undergraduate study followed by two years Masters and three years doctoral work) has already had an influence on the expectations and the mindset of students embarking on study at higher education level. This is particularly so in countries which have witnessed changes to their system of higher education as a result of the Bologna Process. There is already evidence of students in some countries expecting to do Bachelors/Masters/doctoral study, particularly where social work education has been outside the university sector (demonstrated, for example, by an increase in numbers of Belgian, Dutch and German students applying to MACESS). This trend would seem to indicate that in future, there will be a greater demand for postgraduate courses generally, as the currency of higher education shifts in response. Where Bachelor degrees become commonplace, the need for postgraduate and doctoral provision will expand.

The Erasmus Mundus programme

The Erasmus Mundus programme, which was adopted by the European Parliament and Council in December 2003, carries the possibility of opening up European postgraduate programmes to a global audience by financially supporting programmes over a five-year period to encourage students and staff from 'third countries', that is, from outside the EU, EFTA and current applicant countries, to participate in European higher education. The Erasmus Mundus programme initially covers the period 2004 to 2008 and has a budget of €230 million. It will provide: structural funding for European Joint Masters courses to enable them to provide facilities to take students from third countries; third-country student and academic staff scholarships; funding to create third-country partnerships; and measures to enhance the attractiveness of European higher education globally in a number of ways, for example through the recognition of European academic qualifications. While there are some concerns about broadening the courses to students unfamiliar with the European context, Erasmus Mundus is attempting to encourage course providers to develop the European curriculum more within its global context as well as enabling participating programmes to develop an appropriate infrastructure to facilitate mobility (see http://europa.eu.int/comm/education/programmes/mundus/index_en.html, accessed 13/05/04). It appears that the programme hopes to provide a challenge to the prominent position of the US as a global provider of higher education.

Conclusion

This chapter has explored the diversity of European postgraduate provision for the social professions by providing examples of courses that have used a variety of models and funding sources to develop programmes that focus on a range of academic and practice areas at qualifying and post-qualifying levels.

The examples given demonstrate the different structures and patterns of delivery, the variety of curricula addressed to different audiences on different topics and the varied subject focus of the programmes. Commonalities include the involvement of networks, many arising out of EU programmes and projects; funding issues; problems associated with recognition of the award; academic currency (for example Masters programmes may not give automatic access to doctoral study in every country); and, apart from one programme (Berlin) where the focus is on practice, the prominent place of research is a part of the postgraduate curriculum, usually preceding a dissertation.

The development of the Bologna Process to promote harmonisation and recognition could be beneficial to these European programmes as their graduates seek to use their awards in different European countries to further their academic goals and career paths. The sustainability of the European postgraduate programmes is linked to staff and student mobility and funding, including whether more permanent funding streams can be utilised. The incorporation of Joint European Masters programmes into Erasmus Mundus has the potential to open up these programmes to a wider global audience while providing funding to support such an initiative over a five-year period. Undoubtedly, the lessons learnt by and from these programmes will have an impact on the published outcomes, the knowledge base and the practice of social work, as well as increasing the numbers of European research-minded social professionals.

Chapter 8

Imagining the future

Karen Lyons and Sue Lawrence

Introduction

We conclude our discussion of current developments and issues in relation to education for social professionals with a chapter that picks up on some of the points from previous chapters but which also speculates about future possibilities. We have already indicated that we assume that there is an inevitable relationship between developments in education for the social professions and policy change in relation to social services and welfare policies more generally. We consider that education (in its broadest terms, including research) should both reflect and inform such policy and practice developments. Similarly, we have confirmed the view that welfare policies themselves need to be increasingly viewed in the context of regional (European) as well as national political and economic challenges and ambitions.

We have suggested that, for many countries in the region, the European Union (EU) is the main body driving regional policies and that, as well as having direct effects for members states, these may also impact on neighbouring and more distant countries which have either chosen not to join the EU or have not yet attained membership. Additionally, there are other bodies, such as the Council of Europe, which draw the boundaries of Europe more broadly or which focus on more specific activities, whose goals and actions also have implications for countries in the region. However, it is increasingly acknowledged that continental regions and the countries within them are also being influenced by policies and events that have a global dimension, and we therefore pay attention in this concluding chapter to this additional dimension in policies and trends relevant to the social welfare field.

We identify migration as a worldwide phenomenon with significant implications for the demographic and cultural composition of national populations and thus for welfare developments across Europe, and take the increased mobility of labour in the social professional field, itself, as an example of wider trends. In this context we question how far EU aspirations such as 'convergence' of educational programmes and systems and the creation of a European identity are appropriate and attainable, and re-evaluate the role of comparative research and joint educational programmes in promoting 'Europeanisation'. Professional mobility obviously has particular implications for education and regulation, which are considered. We conclude with some thoughts about the role of social professionals in influencing the social agenda and suggest that social professionals oriented to a wider Europe through education, research and practice opportunities, have a significant part to play. Additionally, we recognise the international influences impacting on national practices and the tendencies to localisation that must also be critically attended to at all stages of professional education and development.

Europe in the world: new challenges to the social professions

The term 'globalisation' has recently been much in use although there are ongoing debates about its meaning and its relevance to some populations and occupational groups. An early use of the term described it as 'the process by which previously discreet societies come into contact with and influence each other' (Modelski, 1972, cited in Richards, 1997, p. 19). More recently the notion of 'influence' has perhaps been superseded by the recognition of global 'interdependence' (see later). Richards (1997) went on to suggest that 'globalisation' has many meanings and that these in part reflect the perspective of the user, including the compression of time and place (enabled by technological and transport revolutions), the spread of dominant cultures (including use of the English language), as well as 'the triumph of free trade and the development of global corporations and markets' (Lyons, 1999a, p. 5, paraphrasing Richards, 1997). Midgley (2000), while noting the importance of economic activities and effects, also recognised globalisation as having 'social, political, cultural, demographic and other dimensions as well' (pp.13–14).

Economic features are the ones most frequently associated with globalisation (see, for instance, Michie, 2003) and the effects of economic decisions by trans-national corporations are most likely to impact adversely on people who are already vulnerable, whether in Europe or elsewhere. However, it can seem that populations in countries such as India or China benefit from some current trends at the expense of those in some European countries, for example in the relocation of manufacturing industries or the establishment of call centres. Increases in unemployment figures and in the numbers of people on the margins of otherwise wealthy countries thus pose challenges to European governments to review their economic and financial strategies, with effects on welfare spending and implications for social professionals.

Another aspect related to the notion of interdependence is the gradual recognition that patterns of behaviour in one country or part of the world can have profound implications for whole populations in other societies or perhaps even globally. There are signs of a growing recognition that we inhabit 'one world', not least in relation to resources and the environment, and that consumption levels as well as legislative and technical capabilities in one country can affect the welfare of people in neighbouring or even distant countries. An early example of this was provided in Europe itself, in the effects of the explosion at the nuclear power station at Chernobyl (in Belarus in 1986), polluting land and water in the locality (with the after-effects still being felt, see Bamford, 2001) and spreading airborne pollution well beyond national borders. Other forms of pollution (including excessive oil and gas emissions by rich nations) are destroying local ecosystems but also contributing to global climate change. Lyons (1999a) has discussed the connection between the natural world and 'man-made disasters' and the relevance of environmental concerns to the social work task; and this theme has also been emphasised in a recent Policy Statement by the International Federation of Social Workers (IFSW, 2004). As well as the potentially direct role of social professionals in responding to disasters, we suggest that social workers also need to link up with other bodies aiming to affect environmental policies, whether at national or regional/international levels.

A third aspect of global interdependence rests on the interconnections established between communities in different societies, related to migration patterns that have been shaped, in part, by former empire-building strategies and colonial policies. Castles (2000) identified the racialised nature of colonisation as being a significant feature of this process, with 'white' domination of 'black' or 'Indian' communities. The legacy of colonialism (in terms of the existing relationships between different countries) is reflected demographically in the existence of both long-established minority ethnic populations and in some of the more recent arrivals in many European countries. The extents to which such minority populations have felt 'accepted' and integrated (having equal status and opportunities under the law and in relation to access to employment and to public and private provisions) or have continued to feel subject to overt or covert racism varies greatly across Europe. Concern about race relations and the effectiveness or otherwise of multicultural policies have assumed greater significance since the attack on the World Trade Centre (New York, 11 September 2001); and there is some evidence that perceived injustices and a gulf in religious beliefs (specifically between Judeo-Christian and Muslim traditions) have increased the sense of vulnerability and/or antagonism experienced by both host communities and minority groups (Lyons et al., forthcoming). However, continuing interconnections can be noted in the remittances sent to families 'back home' by minority ethnic communities and also by the larger donations of emigrants for (re)development projects (for example, restoration of some of Kiev's religious buildings by donations from Ukranians living in Canada and the US). Funding and expertise to assist in the development of social services also show trans-Atlantic (in addition to intra-European) tendencies, as for example in the case of a social services project (Veritas Sighisoara) established in Romania with input from American personnel and volunteers (Patterson, 2004).

While globalisation can be said to have superseded colonisation (although it may be a source of other forms of 'colonisation' and exploitation), it is currently proceeding in parallel with other processes at regional and local levels. Thus, as evident in the focus of this book, policies framing social work activities may be regional and the EU is but one example of the way individual states have sought alliances with neighbouring countries – with different regional groupings coming together for different reasons and taking different forms. The relationship between such arrangements and globalisation is variable since some of the regional bodies, notably the predecessor bodies of the EU, were established before the onset of globalisation. The way in which globalisation might impact on the European project was explored nearly a decade ago by Trevillion (1997). It can be argued that regionalism (including the EU) now partly operates as a form of defence against the influence of one superpower (as the US has now become) or against the worst effects of the economic and cultural aspects of globalisation (and perhaps both), as well as aiming to provide a 'counterweight' to these pressures. The extent to which such regional bodies have a direct influence on welfare policies and the role of social professionals varies, with the EU demonstrating a stronger influence and relevance than would be the case in, say, the Asia-Pacific region (Lyons, 1999a).

One of the current challenges to the strength of a regional body such as the EU can be related to its extension from 15 to 25 countries since 2004. This gave rise to various concerns, including that the accession countries would have 'second-class status' (relative to the existing membership); or, conversely, that low labour costs and poorer socioeconomic conditions in the new member states would detract from the benefits of membership previously enjoyed by smaller, peripheral countries (such as Greece, Ireland and Portugal). It is too soon to say whether these 'threats' to stability and growth will materialise. However, a major challenge facing the EU at the time of writing is to convince national voters in some countries of its relevance; to persuade the public that a proposed European constitution is acceptable; and to reduce bureaucracy while promoting more effective democracy. We should also note here the importance of sub-regions in some cases: for instance, the Nordic sub-region has a number of associations and networks that directly involve social professionals or impact on their work (see later).

A similar concern in relation to both globalisation and regionalism is the extent to which the role and power of nation states is affected (see Held et al., 1999, regarding the impact of globalisation). There is some evidence to suggest that an increasing number of countries are influenced by international or regional conventions or directives (such as those emanating from the United Nations [UN] or CoE as well as the EU) in their framing of legislation and development of policy – for instance as regards human rights or services for children – as well as being influenced by dominant political ideologies and economic strictures. The latter pressures are most clearly seen in trends in relation to the welfare state itself and, while recognising the different models that exist within the EU (see Chapter 2), it has been suggested that 'the welfare state' (Mishra, 1999) and even the 'social reform project' (Teeple, 2000) have been adversely affected by the processes of globalisation. In this respect it may be that, at a regional level, values such as solidarity (still strongly held by some of the member states of the EU) have acted as a counterbalance to globalising trends to prevent the worst excesses of marketisation in welfare or to promote policies (such as the minimum wage and family-friendly policies) most likely to benefit people on lower incomes or vulnerable to discriminatory employment practices.

Mention of the nation state also leads us to consideration of the third process, that of 'localisation', closely associated in some cases with the establishment (or reassertion) of national or ethnic identities and perhaps understood as, in part, a reaction against the tendencies towards cultural imperialism (or westernisation) associated with globalisation, as well as being a reaction (in some cases) to regionalism (as represented in the EU) or even the power of the nation state itself. The move towards localisation can take a number of forms, varying from relatively peaceful and only partial (as demonstrated in the devolution of some powers within the UK since 2000 from an English-based Parliament to a Scottish Parliament, a Welsh Assembly and [in due course] a Northern Ireland Assembly) to the more dramatic disintegration of a country such as Yugoslavia in the 1990s and the (re)emergence of a series of smaller countries within the Balkan region.

Such processes and outcomes have presented different opportunities for the development of distinctive social service policies. Variations, for example, are already in evidence in relation to provisions for elder care or social work training, in Scotland relative to England and Wales; and variations are particularly marked in the Balkan region, say between Slovenia (already a member of the EU) and Kosova, still struggling (at the time of writing), with the aid of UN and EU peacekeepers and advisors, to establish a viable political economy, civil society and welfare provisions. Localisation can also refer to a process that takes place within a country, involving the delegation of powers and budgets to administrative units at 'local level', on the assumption that these will be more in touch with local needs and capacities and that resources will be used more effectively if 'managed' in conjunction with local voluntary agencies and community groups. Poland is an example of a country pursuing an active policy of localisation, not least in the development of a range of social care services (Krzyszkowski, 2003). In this case 'localisation' was seen, in part, as a way of 'gearing up' for integration into a regional forum (the EU in 2004) (rather than as a response to globalisation specifically), but in other cases there may be an increased need for people to feel 'connected' to a locality in the face of globalisation.

Returning to the effects of globalisation and some of the issues arising for the EU and member states, we can note that, if information and communication technology and rapid and relatively less expensive transport make it possible for populations living beyond national and regional borders to maintain close and regular contact with home countries, they can also facilitate interconnections that can be used for illegal purposes. Thus, the past decade has seen an increase in trafficking in arms, drugs and people, sometimes within a region, but often across regional boundaries (Lyons et al., forthcoming). Taking the first of these, superficially, arms trafficking would seem to be more of a problem for Africa than Europe. But the extent of armed conflict in Africa has meant that money and effort has been diverted from welfare needs to trying to curb hostilities or assist with physical reconstruction. Additionally, war has been the spur to mass migrations, often to the countries nearest to the site of conflict, but also (for people who could afford it) to European countries. Such movement may deprive the world's poorest countries of some of their better-educated personnel. It also requires major adaptations on the part of those who migrate and they often achieve little positive recognition in a new society. For instance, some are unable to use previous qualifications to full advantage (Lyons, 1999a; and see later).

Drugs have become a major preoccupation of many European governments, causing significant harm to a minority of most national populations and costs to the wider population (for example, through crime, spread of AIDS and related health care costs). Drugs trafficked through major international crimes rings originate from a number of countries (including to the south east of Europe, the Caribbean and South America) and have prompted the growth of international collaboration between law enforcement agencies as well as those concerned with prevention and treatment of drug addiction, or the supervision of people convicted for transporting drugs (drug mules). An example of this is the EU Action Plan on Drugs (2000-04), which includes strengthening the cooperation with the European Monitoring Centre on Drugs and Drug Addiction and Europol, the European law enforcement organisation; developing common definitions, charges and penalties within the EU in the field of drug trafficking; and developing a financial instrument for combating drug trafficking (see www.europarl.eu.int/comparl/libe/elsj/ scoreboard/drugs/default_en.htm, accessed 18/03/05).

People smuggling and trafficking (the distinction is not always clearly drawn, but the latter suggests a more likely use of force) are the most recently recognised forms of cross-border illegal activity, with significant implications for population movement and likely demands on European and national immigration and policing efforts. It can be argued that these activities, particularly trafficking, have negative effects not only on the people ('victims') directly involved (often women and sometimes also children [Manion, 2002]), but that they also affect national perceptions of all immigrants, fuelling distrust and resentment of individuals and minority ethnic communities. Experience in the UK suggests that some of the people smuggled in are from outside the region (including from China and some African countries) but that a significant proportion of people trafficked are from the wider European region, notably the poorer countries of the former Soviet Union, including the Balkan countries (Lyons et al., forthcoming). As with other forms of trafficking, there are complex inter-relations between conditions in the migrants' home countries, individual survival strategies and measures needed to prevent exploitation, corruption and illegality, and there is a need for inter-professional communication and action in devising and implementing effective interventions. However, it seems likely that continued and increased attention needs to be paid to policies and practices that support efforts to promote employment opportunities, community development strategies and other measures (such as the development of civil society and education and training of social work staff) in countries such as Russia and the Ukraine, including through-EU funded partnership initiatives.

The EU has been responding to these challenges (and other effects of globalisation) in a variety of ways. Some strategies can be seen as attempting to assert a counter-balance to US dominance in international affairs (Kaletsky, 2004) with the aim of providing alternative strategies, for example in relation to external military interventions or aid to Africa. However, other efforts are more concerned with promoting internally cohesive policies, some of which impact directly on the work of social professionals. This is perhaps most evident in the field of migration where there are mixed messages about the desirability or otherwise of allowing immigration from outside EU borders. On the one hand, EU policies and most national policies have become noticeably 'tougher', apparently requiring social workers in some countries to become part of the immigration control system (see, for instance, Humphreys [2002] with regard to the UK). On the other hand, there is widespread concern throughout Europe about falling birth rates and the increasing age dependency ratio, and there are signs of some recognition that this demographic problem may be addressed through immigration policies (see, for example, O'Connell 1999; Corkill, 2001; Schneider, 2003), but possibly only in the short term (Cliquet, 2005). However, it is also possible that the recent expansion of the EU and proposed admission of additional new member states in 2007, together with policies on (internal) labour mobility, will enable this issue to be addressed predominantly within EU borders. This may have implications for family reunification, inter-country adoption or other policies affecting third-country nationals.

Reverting briefly to the issue of demographic concerns, these are most frequently expressed in terms of worries about the increasing number of people in national populations over retirement age (with implications for pension provision) and predictions about further rises in the numbers of 'frail elderly' people (causing concern about resources in the health and social care fields) (Walker and Maltby, 1997). These concerns are sometimes expressed in cost terms in wider public arenas, but have also been voiced in the professional press regarding the availability of sufficient numbers of appropriately trained personnel and the standards of care provided in the residential sector (whether through public, private or voluntary agencies) with debates about the role that social professionals should play in this area of work. Reference to availability of staff leads us on to a consideration of a specific aspect of migration, as it occurs in relation to the social professional workforce itself, to which we now turn.

Labour mobility in the social professional field in Europe

One of the early ambitions of the EU was to increase the 'freedom of movement' of people (labour) as well as capital, goods and services (see Chapter 2). Concern about transferability of qualifications in a number of occupations resulted initially in Directives about comparability in specific occupations and then a General Directive in 1989. This applied to all occupations not yet covered but whose members had successfully completed a minimum of three years training in a higher education institution and who were approved (registered) to work in a particular field. This Directive was succeeded by a similar one relating to people qualifying on two-year diplomas (sub-degree level) that covered some social professional qualifications. However, education to undergraduate degree level for at least three years has become increasingly the norm among the social professions in European member states and most national governments have also introduced registration schemes where these did not already exist. General rules at European level have been modified by specific rules and procedures at national levels (Kornbeck, 2004).

Given the need for local knowledge and cultural understanding in the development of services and practice in social work (Webb, 2004), it might be assumed that only locally trained social professionals could operate effectively. However, it has been noted that social work students are as involved in (European) mobility as students in other subject areas (Seibel and Lorenz, 1998), and there is some indication of an increase in mobility of qualified social professionals more recently, although actual data on worker mobility (as opposed to student mobility) is sparse. Kornbeck (2003) reported a survey carried out by the European Liaison Committee of the International Federation of Social Workers (IFSW) in 1997 into labour mobility: its findings suggested that national associations have some anecdotal evidence about their own members working abroad but none about incoming social workers. Meanwhile, a study in 1999 (also cited by Kornbeck, 2003), comparing labour markets across France, Denmark, Germany, Italy, the Netherlands and the UK, concluded that the UK offered the greatest opportunities for employment of social professional graduates because of staff shortages.

In relation to the UK, Sims (2004) reported a survey finding of vacancy rates in 'children and family' teams (in English local authority departments) of 12.6% nationally and over 23% in London at the end of 2002 and, in this context, national debates surrounding comparability of courses and qualifications and registration have taken on particular significance . A central body has been responsible for checking the equivalence of 'overseas qualifications' since the early 1970s and applications to the General Social Care Council (GSCC) have risen considerably in the 21st century. The GSCC processed 2,524 applications in the period April 2003 to May 2004, an increase of 82% on the previous year. This can be compared with a 67% increase in numbers approved between 1991 and 2001, 75% of which were from Anglophone countries (including 67% from Commonwealth countries such as Australia, Canada and South Africa) (Kornbeck, 2004). However, recruits have also come from countries both within and outside the EU, including Sweden and Romania (Sims, 2004). From April 2005, all personnel occupying social work posts must be registered with the GSCC, adding to the cost and complexity of applications from people who qualified abroad and are seeking work in the UK.

It can be noted that, for a period in the 1980s and 1990s, the UK was one of the few countries limiting entry to social work courses (although this no longer applies in such formal terms) and that countries such as Greece, Germany and Spain have for many years produced more social workers (including people with social pedagogy qualifications) than posts that were available. Additionally, it is anticipated that there could also be a surplus of social professionals in some of the Central and Eastern Europe (CEE) countries where significant efforts have been made to (re-)establish social work education programmes but where supply of newly qualified workers might be outstripping demand. This may be partly due to a shortage of funding for posts in voluntary and statutory agencies, since demand (in terms of need for services) is considerable in countries such as Poland and the Ukraine (personal communications). Given the shortage of jobs, as well as generally low wage rates prevalent in the most recent member states of the EU, it seems likely that social workers will be among the professionals expected to take advantage of job opportunities in the UK and possibly other EU countries.

As indicated in Chapter 7, there is already anecdotal evidence that a proportion of students are using post-graduate programmes with a European or international focus as a means of learning about comparative social policies and exploring issues that have cross-national or European dimensions. Among these, some students are gaining part-time work experience 'abroad' or are subsequently entering the workforce on a full-time basis (Lyons, 2004). It is not yet clear whether such staff will see employment in a country other than where they gained their professional qualification as a short-term opportunity to gain experience or as the basis for longer-term resettlement away from their country of origin. However, it is becoming apparent that, whatever the motivations and longer-term intentions of social professionals who migrate, there are policy and practice implications – for the recruitment agencies, for employing authorities and their staff and for the migrant workers themselves (Lawrence, 2005) These are to do with resettlement issues as well as orientation and induction programmes and the longer-term training and supervision needs of people working in different legal, organisational and cultural contexts.

One aspect of 'cultural competence' that has received relatively little attention in the literature (perhaps because it is taken for granted) is the need for proficiency in the relevant national language as a prerequisite for professional intervention. The recruitment of social workers to England from predominantly Anglophone countries would seem to support this view. However, other factors might also be at work in this case, and assumptions that a shared language equips people for other aspects of cultural difference may not hold true. Additionally, the increase in the number of migrants and the variety of their countries of origin pose challenges in some localities to a range of welfare services (in terms of meeting linguistic needs), requiring some social professionals to develop skills in working through interpreters (Sanders, 2003). Kornbeck (2003) has noted the need for greater language proficiency in Spain and Germany where social professionals are also working with increasingly diverse communities. But he has also suggested that lack of language proficiency limits labour mobility, particularly in a field such as social work, and his edited book advocates increased attention to the teaching of language for professional purposes in social work curricula (in all countries), as well as giving examples of curricula.

Alternatively, another response to labour shortages is to review policies that could encourage the development of 'home-grown' resources. In the UK, in parallel with overseas recruitment, more attention is being paid to personnel policies that tap into the local labour force (including through new trainee schemes and improved retention strategies). However, greater efforts need to be made in many countries to offer qualifying programmes to existing minority groups as well as to more recent arrivals, including refugees. Relatively more attention to the 'hidden resource' among asylum seekers has been paid by the health service (also seriously under-staffed) with a growing recognition that some refugees already hold qualifications in the health care field and special programmes (including language training) have been devised to 'fast-track' such people (Kornbeck, 2003). While it may be less likely that refugees will already hold social professional qualifications, some will have gained relevant experience since arrival in the UK through operating as interpreters and advisers for their own communities (Masters, 2003) and they could form a valuable resource for the workforce if offered additional training. Given the number of European countries which have granted asylum to refugees (particularly in the last few years), such a resource is not limited to the UK and other countries such as the Netherlands and Finland are also concerned about how best to capitalise on the skills and qualifications of refugees (personal communication). This strategy must benefit not only individual refugees and the particular minorities from which they are drawn, but also the wider society, given the need for a more diverse workforce better able to respond to multicultural (including multi-faith) communities.

Finally in this section, we consider the efforts of regional or international associations to ensure comparability of standards attained in relation to qualifying courses for social work in different countries. It has already been noted that individual countries have set up their own mechanisms for approving the equivalence of qualifications gained elsewhere and there are some signs that there may be moves away from an 'individual assessment' approach towards a blanket approval of qualifications from one country as equipping social workers to practice in another. (For example, this is being considered by the GSCC in relation to Irish qualifications.) A unifying framework for the disparate occupational groups constituting the social professions has already been advanced by the IFSW and the International Association of Schools of Social Work (IASSW) in the international 'definition' of social work (see Chapter 1) and IASSW had long ago set down criteria that schools seeking membership were required to demonstrate that they met. More recently (2004) the two organisations have agreed a document setting out global standards for social work education (IASSW, 2005).

The arguments for and against producing such a document (as well as the protracted process followed to achieve this outcome) have been discussed by Sewpaul and Jones, (2004) and a number of other authors in a special issue of a British journal, Social Work Education. There are clearly concerns that it might be seen as an (additional) attempt to regulate and homogenise education for social professionals, with the added concern that it is essentially another way in which 'western ideas' will determine how professional education should develop in very different countries. (For example, Yip [2004] has critiqued the document from a Chinese perspective, suggesting that a number of the values stated to be important, such as promotion of rights, change and equality might be at variance with the greater emphasis given in Confucian societies to responsibilities, stability and respect). However, it has also been argued (including by some educators in CEE countries and other places where social work education is relatively newly [re-]established) that it is useful to have an international set of standards by which to 'measure' progress and as a basis for negotiations with officials in higher education and ministries about what is expected, internationally.

Whether defining social work at an international level and issuing a statement of aspirations about global qualifying standards is broadly regarded as useful across the range of European countries remains to be seen, but the journal also carried an article (Juliusdottir and Petersson, 2004), which discussed the difficulty of agreeing standards even at a sub-regional level. The authors presented the situation in the Nordic region and identified two major dimensions of difference evident between qualifying programmes in the Nordic countries. They described these as educational programmes based on the view of social work as essentially a vocational subject in which experience plays a significant part (as, for example, in Norway) relative to a view that social work can be developed from a more academic base, with considerable emphasis put on research (as, for example, in Finland). These two perspectives are evident in debates about the development of social work education even within a country (such as the UK) and perhaps even more so in countries where different qualifications are increasingly recognised as having equal value (such as in Germany in relation to the *sozial arbeit/sozial pedagog* debate). Whether global standards in themselves will brings us closer to harmonisation of standards across Europe remains to be seen.

Additionally, whether global standards (or even an element of regulation and accreditation of courses at a European level, as has been proposed by the European Association of Schools of Social Work), brings us any nearer to something that could be called 'European social work' is a moot point. However, the 'European project' (including through Erasmus and Socrates programmes) has been important in helping many social professionals to recognise shared values and commonalities in knowledge and skills, at an operational level, and also the way in which social problems are either similar across borders or do literally cross national borders. Such learning has strengthened awareness of the need for common understandings based on similar or even shared educational programmes and we shall now turn to the implications of the foregoing for educational developments.

Implications for education of social professionals

The Erasmus Mundus programme (see Chapter 7) has provided some evidence of an acknowledgement, at European level, that the EU and its member states do not operate in isolation from the rest of the world. While the political motivation behind this policy may lie in concerns about the competitiveness of European institutions in preparing people for the knowledge society, it nevertheless provides an opportunity for postgraduate courses to enable social professionals to extend their knowledge and understanding of global as well as regional trends and of events and cultures beyond Europe, which impact locally. A related move by the EU to encourage courses leading to joint awards at postgraduate level across national borders currently presents universities in a number of countries with difficulties (related to a perceived loss of autonomy as well as concerns about how to ensure equivalent standards) but anecdotal evidence from England suggests that some universities are actively engaging with this development.

Additionally, social work schools in some countries, such as Sweden, already offer opportunities (through electives and placement opportunities) for students to explore both regional and global perspectives at the qualifying stage. Increased awareness of the global nature of some problems, as well as the regional efforts to address them, challenge all those educating social professionals to consider how best to incorporate European and international dimensions in their own programmes. Useful lessons have been learned from previous engagement in the Erasmus and Socrates programmes (see Chapters 6 and 7) and these provide a basis for new developments rooted in established and new cross-national networks. While the need for increased attention to language training may be a specific curriculum requirement, the possibility of arranging for students to undertake placements or project work in another country has been enhanced by the gradual increase in the number of people now working in the social professions who have themselves had exposure to European or international courses or placements.

Additionally, there are a number of shared concerns across European borders that could provide a focus for collaborative efforts in research, short course development (intensive programmes), and common electives or optional modules (jointly developed but offered in different countries) as well as the possibility of whole courses leading to joint awards. A number of issues can be identified as possible areas for curriculum development in all qualifying courses, with scope for more in-depth attention in specialist (postgraduate) programmes. However, perhaps a useful starting point in relation to any new developments in professional education is to return to the fundamental question – 'What are we aiming to educate social workers for?' – but to re-evaluate this question, not just in the light of local concerns and requirements, but also in the context of regional and international trends and frameworks. The IASSW and IFSW have offered a necessarily abstract 'definition' of social work but this can be 'unpacked' in relation to its meaning(s) in a given place as well as drawing on material (or gathering new material) about how this plays out in another place. In this way, courses that offer opportunities for comparative learning provide a valuable insight into cultural and other differences informing social service provision as well as prompting a critical appreciation of domestic systems.

It is possible to identify a number of relatively 'new social issues' with European or international dimensions, which are now apparent in practice and which, it could be argued, social professionals should be 'trained' to address. Examples include the rise in child pornography on the internet and commercial sexual exploitation of children (both of which sometimes have cross-border aspects); the increased opportunities for inter-country adoption or the possibility that national policies in relation to kinship care will require trans-national placement; the plight of asylum seekers – or young women who have been trafficked – whose experiences (including in their new destinations) have left them vulnerable to physical ill health or mental health problems (and for whom employment prospects seem limited); and the particular needs of elderly migrants who have become 'stranded' away from their country of origin. All of these might be the subject of research or intensive programmes that aim to analyse the problem from a range of perspectives and consider possible responses (at individual, group and community level) in different countries or at the European level.

However, while attention to 'new issues' in a fairly discreet way is an appropriate approach to research and intensive programmes – and will always be an aspect of qualifying education (for example through student field placements or project work) – there is a danger, in relation to qualifying education, that such an approach merely leads to a sense of an overfull curriculum or one that is focusing on intervention in relation to some user groups at the expense of others. It therefore seems important to equip students with knowledge of the fundamental issues underlying specific social problems (for instance, as related to poverty, migration and environmental concerns) and some of the overarching international frameworks and regional and national policies that are in place to address them. Building on this knowledge base, Ife (2001) has identified the need for more social professionals to engage in a macro-analysis of oppression and disadvantage and to give attention to national and international policies and frameworks (and we would add, regional) as well as local contextual knowledge and initiatives.

These suggestions require (some) social professionals to go beyond the implementation of selected social policies (which many see as their role) in relation to individuals (or groups or communities) locally to playing a greater part in identifying gaps and malfunctioning in national and international policies, and developing their skills in advocacy and lobbying for social change at structural levels. Orientating social professionals to these roles would require a paradigm shift in the form and content of social work education in some countries, since it reintroduces a more political dimension to the role of social professionals. We are not suggesting that all social professionals will become 'activists' in policy forums, nor that all will operate at European or international levels. However, we consider that there needs to be the capacity within the profession as a whole for some professionals to engage in these roles, for instance through the agency of national associations or European/international organisations. Such efforts – to take seriously the 'change' (as opposed to amelioration) role of social professionals – can be facilitated by (re)connecting with other professionals and agencies, including civil associations and movements with similar concerns.

How might the foregoing idea fit with trends (widely recognised in a number of European countries) towards increased regulation of social workers in agencies where managerialism and increasingly bureaucratic procedures seem designed to prevent any opportunity to consider wider perspectives, make connections or introduce innovation in local practice? Perhaps we can learn from Australian experience, where social work education has expanded (in terms of the number of courses offered and numbers qualifying) but where it is not expected that all graduates go into posts labelled as 'social work' in local authority/state services (Crisp, 2003). All students undertake a broadly based education on a four-year degree and individuals have the opportunity to undertake electives/optional modules and a wide range of placements (which might include, for instance, the 'surgery' of a local politician or the planning office of a Ministry). In this sense the use of the term 'social professional' in Europe already suggests the recognition of a range of routes to related qualifications, all equipping people to work in the social field, utilising similar values and theoretical knowledge but having different emphases, including engaging with different levels of the local and wider social systems.

Additionally, the idea of the portfolio career – where people take on different roles in different organisations, perhaps also including periods of work as 'self-employed' – which is now widespread and sometime seen as a threat to individual job security in the world of work generally, might be seen as a positive opportunity for social professionals. The term 'transferable skills' is already familiar to many engaged in professional education (not least in the Australian example quoted) and increased regulation also brings the expectation of 'continuing professional development'. Potentially this could offer scope for learning new skills and changing direction within the wider professional field. In this context, there are also signs of increased mobility of social professionals, not just in the form of temporary or permanent migration discussed above but also in the willingness of some social workers to leave or step out of their usual jobs (perhaps for up to a year) to take on work (sometimes as a volunteer or as a consultant) outside their home country (see, for instance, King, 2004). There are therefore already some indications of both the need for, and the resources to enable, developments in professional education that are informed by European and international perspectives.

Concluding comments

We have aimed in this book to analyse and illustrate some of the ways in which developments in education for the social professions have been, and need to be increasingly, informed by knowledge of European policies and frameworks. We have also suggested that many social issues can now be seen to have cross-national dimensions and that social professionals increasingly need some appreciation of comparative perspectives to facilitate effective practice and service developments. Additionally, the lives of individuals and communities with whom social professionals engage are increasingly affected by global events and processes as well as by trends evident at regional and national levels. Starting from a different (European) perspective, we would therefore extend Ife's (2001) call for a global-local dialect to include a regional level of analysis and intervention.

This thematic examination of education and research for social professionals in Europe reveals both some consistencies (for example, in the values underlying practice, the social issues identified as problematic and some of the issues for social work educators themselves) and some diversity (notably in the organisational and legislative bases for social services) as reflected in different educational programmes and qualifications. A major factor underlying differences in approaches to welfare and to the education of social professions is rooted in national histories and cultures, and the latter are only gradually adapting to, or being changed by, migration patterns both within the EU and from outside its borders. Despite this, some see globalisation as posing a threat in the form of cultural homogenisation; and the increase in the range of international conventions and statements that seek to provide frameworks for national developments (including the global standards for social work education) similarly might suggest universalising tendencies. Additionally, the EU itself is sometimes perceived as a threat to the autonomy of member states, including in relation to welfare and higher education policies.

While a comparative study of social professional activity and associated educational provisions might not as yet reveal strong signs of convergence, we suggest that social professionals across Europe need to be prepared for similar tasks associated with societal change and have a part to play in identifying developments that might threaten individual and collective identities, relative to policies that enhance mutual respect and promote human rights and social justice. In addition, a number of social professionals are learning experientially, whether as students or as workers, about the personal challenges and opportunities presented in crossing borders and are developing identities and affiliations that may transcend a mono-cultural or exclusively national self. We conclude that all social professionals can be assisted to develop a fuller appreciation of the possibilities and responsibilities related to practice and service developments in the 21st century through enhanced opportunities to learn about European and international as well as local policies and practices.

Appendix:
European and International protocols relevant to Anti-Racist Social Work

a) European Conventions and other protocols

- Amsterdam Treaty, Article 13
- Directive 2000/43 passed by the Council of the European Union on 29 June 2000 to implement the principle of equal treatment between persons irrespective of racial or ethnic origin.
- European Charter for Regional or Minority Languages
- European Charter of Fundamental Rights
- European Convention for the Prevention of Torture and Inhuman or Degrading Treatment or Punishment
- European Convention for the Protection of Human Rights and Fundamental Freedoms
- European Convention on Human Rights (ECHR)
- European Convention on Nationality
- European Convention on the Legal Status of Migrant Workers
- European Convention on the Participation of Foreigners in Public Life at Local Level
- European Social Charter and the Revised European Social Charter
- Framework Convention for the Protection of National Minorities
- Framework Convention for the Protection of National Minorities
- Framework Directive on Discrimination in Employment

b) International Conventions and other protocols

- 1951 Geneva Convention on Refugees
- 1967 Protocol on Status of Refugees
- Convention Against Torture and Other Cruel, Inhuman or Degrading Treatment (CAT)
- Convention of the Elimination of All Forms of Discrimination against Women (CEDAW), including the Option Protocol
- Convention on the Prevention and Punishment of the Crime of Genocide
- Convention on the Protection of the Rights of All Migrant Workers and Members of their Families, 1990
- Convention on the Rights of the Child (CRC) (articles 2 on non-discrimination and 22 on refugee children)
- Convention on the Status of Stateless Persons, 1954
- ILO Convention Concerning Discrimination (Employment and Occupation)
- ILO Convention on Indigenous and Tribal Peoples
- ILO Declaration on Fundamental Principles and Rights at Work
- International Convention against Transnational Organised Crime (trafficking in people and smuggling of migrants)
- International Convention on Civil and Political Rights (ICCPR), including the First Optional Protocol
- International Convention on the Elimination of All Forms of Racial Discrimination (ICERD)
- International Covenant on Economic, Social and Cultural Rights (ICESCR), including the Optional Protocol
- The Rome Statute of the International Criminal Court
- UN Declaration on the Rights of National, Ethnic, Religious and Linguistic Minorities
- UNESCO Convention against Discrimination in Education
- Universal Declaration of Human Rights
- World Conference Against Racism in 2001 in Durban

References

Abye, T (2001) 'Social work with migrants and refugees in France' in Dominelli, L, Lorenz, W and Soydan, H (eds) *Beyond Racial Divides: Ethnicities in social work practice*, Aldershot, Ashgate

Abye, T (2003) 'Ethiopian migrants in France and the United States', Ph D Thesis, Paris, Ecole Pratique des Sciences Sociales

Adams, A and Shardlow, S (2000) 'Social work practice in the United Kingdom' in Adams, A, Erath, P and Shardlow, S (eds) *Fundamentals of Social Work in Selected European Countries: Historical and political context, present theory, practice, perspectives,* Lyme Regis, Russell House Publishing, pp 119–38

Adams, A and Shardlow, S (2002) 'The fruits of a European partnership' *Social Work in Europe,* 9(2), pp 50–55

Adams, R, Erath, P and Shardlow, S (eds) (2000) *Key Themes in European Social Work.* Lyme Regis, Russell House Publishing

Adams, R, Erath, P and Shardlow, S (eds) (2001) *Fundamentals of Social Work in Selected European Countries.* Lyme Regis, Russell House Publishing

Ahmad, B (1990) *Black Perspectives in Social Work.* Birmingham, Venture Press

Aabro, C (2004) 'The Common Third', written communication with author

Allan, T (2003) 'Ethical issues in social work research', Paper presented to ESRC-sponsored workshop for PhD students, Bradford, UK, 6 March

Altmeyer, A (1955) 'Training for international responsibilities' in Myrdal, A, Altmeyer, A and Rusk, D (eds) *America's Role in International Social Welfare* New York, Columbia University Press

Aluffi-Pentini, A and Lorenz, W (eds) (1996) *Anti-Racist Work with Young People: European experiences and approaches.* Lyme Regis, Russell House Publishing

Amin, A (2003) *From Ethnicity to Empathy: A new idea of Europe.* Open Democracy, 24 July, www.openDemocracy.net

Anders-Dropping, J, Hvinden, B and Vik, K (1999) 'Activation policies in the Nordic Countries' in Kautto, M, Hiekila, M, Hvinden, B, Marklund, S and Ploug N (eds) *Nordic Social Policy: Changing welfare states* London, Routledge, pp 133–53.

Asante, M (1987) *The Africentric Idea* Philadelphia, Templeton University Press

Back, L and Nayak, A (eds) (1998) *Invisible Europeans? Black people in the 'New Europe'* London, Routledge

Baistow, K (2000) 'Cross-national research: What can we learn from inter-country comparisons?' *Social Work in Europe*, 7(3), pp 8–13

Bamford, M. (2001) 'Why not buy a cow?' *Professional Social Work*, December, pp 10–11

Bamford, D and Ross, J (2003) 'A challenge in Transylvania: Part II: The Sequel' *Social Work in Europe*, 10(2), pp 23–31

Bamford, D, Coposescu, S and Ross, J (2000) 'A challenge in Transylvania: Major issues associated with creating a postgraduate social work course in Romania' *Social Work in Europe*, 7(2), pp 8–17

Barker, M (1981) *The New Racism: Conservatives and the ideology of the tribe* London: Junction Books

Beck, U (1992) Risk Society: *Towards a new modernity* London, Sage Publications

Berlin Communiqué (2003) 'Communiqué of the Conference of Ministers Responsible for Higher Education', Press Release from the European Commission, Berlin, 19 September

Berry, J W, Poortinga, Y H, Segall, M H and Dasen, P R (2002) *Cross-Cultural Psychology: Research and applications* (2nd edition) Cambridge, Cambridge University Press

Berthelsen, J, Clod, P, Steen, J and Illeris, K (1996) *Grundbog I projektarbejde: Teori og praktisk vejledning* Copenhagen, Unge Paedagoger

Bjorgo, T and White, R (1993) *Racist Violence in Europe* London, Macmillan

Cheles, L, Ferguson, R and Vaughan, M (1991) *Neo-Fascism in Europe* Harlow, Longman

Boddy, J, Cameron, C, Hepinstall, E, McQuail, J and Petrie, P (2003) *Working with Children: Social pedagogy and residential child care in Europe* (draft report) London, Department of Health

Borghill, L (2004) 'The empowerment of young people at risk through sport and outdoor activities', Unpublished undergraduate dissertation, University of Portsmouth, UK

Boswell, C (2002) *EU Immigration and asylum policy: From Tampere to Laeken and beyond* RIIA Briefing Paper (New Series) 30, London, Royal Institute for International Affairs, www.riia.org

Brah A (2001) 'Re-framing Europe: gendered racisms, ethnicities and nationalisms in contemporary Western Europe' in Fink, J, Lewis, G and Clarke, J (eds) *Rethinking European Welfare* London, Sage Publications

Brandon, D, Khoo, R, Ambler, S, Maglajlik, R, Stevenson, A and Abuel-Ealeh, M (1998) 'European snapshot survey of attitudes to mental health' *Breakthrough*, 2(2), pp 5–20

Brauns, H J and Kramer, D (eds) (1986) *Social Work Education in Europe: A comprehensive description of social work education in 21 European countries* Frankfurt, Eigenverlag des Deutschen Vereins für öffentliche und private Fürsorge

Buckley, H (2003) *Child Protection Work: Beyond the rhetoric* London, Jessica Kingsley Publishers

Butler, I (2002) 'Critical commentary: A code of ethics for social work and social care research' *British Journal of Social Work*, 32(2), pp 239–48

Cannan, C, Berry, L and Lyons, K (1992) *Social Work and Europe* Basingstoke, BASW/Macmillan

Castles, F (2001) 'On the political economy of recent public sector development' *Journal of European Social Policy*, 11(3), pp 195–211

Castles, S (2000) *Ethnicity and Globalization* London, Sage Publications

Cheles, L, Ferguson, R and Vaughan, M (1991) *Neo-Fascism in Europe* Harlow, Longmans

Christopherson, R J (1998) 'Social work students' perceptions of child abuse: An international comparison and post-modern interpretation of its findings' *British Journal of Social Work*, 28(1), pp 57–72

Chytil, O (2002) 'In brief: Social work history in the Czech Republic', Summary and translation by Necasova, M *Bulletin of European Association of Schools of Social Work*, 8 February.

Chytil, O and Seibel, F W (eds) (1999) *European Dimensions in Training and Practice of Social Professions* Papers from Erasmus Thematic Network Conference, Ostrava, 1998, Blansko, Albert

Chytil, O, Lorenz, W, Seibel, F W and Striezenec, S (eds) (2000) *Building on Experience: Preparing the social professions for tomorrow's Europe* Papers from the Erasmus Thematic Network Conference, Modra, 1999, Blansko, Albert

Clarke J (2001) 'Globalization and welfare states: some unsettling thoughts' in Sykes, R, Palier, B and Prior, P (eds) *Globalization and Welfare States: Challenges and change* Basingstoke, Palgrave, pp 19–37

Clarke, J (2004) *Changing Welfare, Changing States: New directions in social policy* London, Sage Publications

Cliquet, R (2005) 'Population issues and social cohesion: priorities for action', Paper presented to the European Population Conference: Demographic Challenges for Social Cohesion, Strasbourg, Council of Europe, April

CoE (Council of Europe) (1994) *Report on Racism, Xenophobia, Anti-Semitism and Intolerance in Europe*, Strasbourg, CoE

Constable, R and Mehta, V (eds) (1994) *Education for Social Work in Eastern Europe: Changing horizons* Chicago, Lyceum Press

Cooper, A (1992) 'Anxiety and child protection in two national systems' *Journal of Social Work Practice*, 6(2), pp 117–28

Corbett, A (2003) 'Europe: a threat or an opportunity for higher education?', Paper presented to the Society for Research in Higher Education Conference: 'The White Paper and the Bologna Agreement – are they compatible?', London, 7 March

Corkill, D (2001) 'Economic migrants and the labour market in Spain and Portugal' *Ethnic and Racial Studies*, 24(5), pp 828–44

Cornwall, N (1994) 'Social work education and practice sans frontiers' *Issues in Social Work Education*, 14(1), pp 39– 52

Courtioux, M, Davies Jones, H, Kalcher, J, Steinhauser, W, Tuggener, H and Waaldijk, K (1984) At *Leve Med Andre Som Erhverv Socialpedagog I Europa* Denmark, Federation Internationale des Communautes d'Enfants

Crisp, B (2003) 'Similar but not the same: social work education in Britain from an Australian perspective' in Littlechild, B and Lyons, K (eds) (2003) *Locating the Occupational Space for Social Work: International perspectives* BASW Monograph, Expanding Horizons in Social Work and Allied Professions, Birmingham, Venture Press

Curry, L, Wergin, J F and Associates (1993) *Educating Professionals: Responding to new expectations for competence and accountability* San Francisco, Jossey Bass

Dal Pra Ponticelli, M (2001) 'La riforma universitaria di fronte alla sfida del nuovo assistente sociale' in Sgroi, E, Rizza, S and Gui, L (eds) *Rapporto sulla situazione del servizio sociale* Rome, EISS, pp 273–77

Danbolt, T and Askeland, G (2004) Changes in social work education in Norway, *European Journal of Social Work*, 7(3), pp 355–8

De Vita, G (2002) 'Cultural equivalence in the assessment of home and international business management students: A UK exploratory study' *Studies in Higher Education*, 27(2), pp 221–231

Deacon, B (2000) 'East European welfare states: The impact of the politics of globalization' *Journal of European Social Policy*, 10(2), pp 146–61

Delanty, G (1995) *Inventing Europe* Basingstoke, Macmillan

Delanty, G. (2000) *Citizenship in a Global Age* Buckingham, Open University Press

Dellgran, P and Höjer, S (2003) 'Topics and epistemological positions in Swedish social work research' *Social Work Education*, 22(6), pp 565–75

Der Boghossian, A (2003) 'A question of political will?' *Connections*, Winter 2003/04, London, Commission for Racial Equality

Dobrev, S (2003) 'Therapeutic change' *Orbit*, (VSO), 87, pp 6–7

Doel, M and Shardlow, S (eds) (1996) *Social Work in a Changing World: An international perspective on practice learning*, Aldershot, Arena

Dominelli, L (1988) *Anti-Racist Social Work* London, Macmillan, second edition published in 1997, third edition in press

Dominelli, L (1995) 'Anti-racist perspectives in social work education: a model for practice' in Dominelli, L, Patel, N and Thomas Bernard, W (eds) *Anti-Racist Social Work Education: Models for practice* Sheffield, Department of Sociological Studies, Sheffield University

Dominelli, L (2000) 'Tackling racism in everyday realities: a task for social workers' in Callahan, M, Hessle, V and Strega, S (eds) *Valuing the Field: Child welfare in an international context* Aldershot, Ashgate

Dominelli, L (2001) 'Anti-oppressive practice in context' in Adams, R, Dominelli, L and Payne, M (eds) *Social Work: Themes, Issues and Critical Debates* London, Palgrave

Dominelli, L (2002) *Anti-Oppressive Social Work Theory and Practice* London, Palgrave

Dominelli, L (2004a) *Social Work: Theory and practice for a changing profession* Cambridge, Polity Press

Dominelli, L (2004b) 'Culturally competent social work: a way toward international anti-racist social work?' in Gutiérrez, L, Zuniga, M and Lum, D (eds) *Education for Multicultural Social Work Practice: Critical viewpoints and future directions*, Alexandria, VA, Council for Social Work Education

Dominelli, L and Hoogvelt, A (1996) 'Globalisation and the technocratisation of social work' *Critical Social Policy*, 47, 16(2), pp 45–62

Düvell, F. and Jordan, B. (2002) 'Immigration, asylum and welfare' *Critical Social Policy*, 22(3), pp 498–517

EC (European Commission) (1993) *European Social Policy: Options for the future*, Green Paper, Luxembourg, EC

EC (1994) *European Social Policy: A way forward for the Union*, Luxembourg, EC

EC (2005) http://europa.eu.int/comm/education/programmes/socrates/erasmus/erasmus_en.html, accessed 17 August 2005

Edwards, R and Boreham, N (2003) 'The centre cannot hold: complexity and difference in EU policy towards a learning society' *Journal of Education Policy*, 18(4), pp 407–21

Elections (2004) www.elections2004.eu.int/ep-election/sites/en/results1306/turnout_ep/index.html, accessed 17/08/05

Elsen, S (2004) 'Schöne neue (Hochschul-) Welt: Anmerkungen zur Reform der europäischen Hochschullandschaft' in Steinmetz, B, Elsen, S and Seibel, F W (eds) *Der Bologna-Prozess in Europa, eine Herausforderung für die Ausbildung in der Sozialen Arbeit in Deutschland*, Weimar, Bertuch, pp 43–50

Esping-Andersen, G (1990) *The Three Worlds of Welfare Capitalism* Cambridge, Polity

Essed, P (1991) *Understanding Everyday Racism: An interdisciplinary theory* London, Sage Publications

EUA (European University Association) (2002) *Joint Masters Project: Call for applications to interested networks* Brussels, EUA

EUA (2003) Press release, 23 April, Brussels

EUMC (European Monitoring Centre on Racism and Xenophobia) (2005) *Report on Racism and Xenophobia in Europe* Brussels, EUMC

Europa (2005a) http://europa.eu.int/comm/education/policies.educ/bologna/bologna_en.html, accessed 17/08/05

Europa (2005b) http://europa.eu.int/comm/education/policies/2010/et_2010_en.html, accessed 17/08/05

Fink, J, Lewis, G and Clarke, J (2001) *Rethinking European Welfare* London, Sage Publications/Oxford University Press

Flem, A L (2004) *Teaching Social Work from North to South: Professional Imperialism or Mutual Professional Development* Trondheim, Sør Trøndelag University College, Faculty of Health Education and Social Work

Fook, J (2002) *Social Work: Critical theory and practice* London, Sage Publications

Förster, M and Pearson, M (2002) *Income Distribution and Poverty in the OECD Area* OECD Economic Studies No 34, Paris, Organisation for Economic Co-operation and Development, www.oecd.org

Foucault, M (1980) *Power/Knowledge: Selected interviews and other writings, 1972–77* New York, Pantheon Books

Frankenburg, R (1997) *Displacing Whiteness: Essays in social and cultural criticism* London, Duke University Press

Freire, P (1972) *Pedagogy of the Oppressed* Harmondsworth, Penguin

Freitas, M J (2004) 'The Netherlands' in Campanini, A and Frost E (eds) *European Social Work: Commonalities and differences* Rome, Carocci, pp 153–61

French, M (1985) *The Power of Women* Harmondsworth, Penguin

Froslund, M, Jergeby, U, Soydan, H and Williams, C (2002) 'Responding to ethnicity: A cross-national evaluation of social work responses in child protection cases' *Social Work in Europe*, 9(3), pp 39–52

Geddes, A (2000) *Immigration and European Integration* Manchester, Manchester University Press

Giddens, A (1990) *The Consequences of Modernity* Cambridge, Polity Press

Ginsburg, N (1996) *Social Europe – A new model of welfare?* London, University of North London for London European Research Centre

Gordon, G (1980) *Michael Foucault Power/Knowledge: Selected interviews and other writings 1972–1977* London, Harvester Wheatsheaf

Gordon, P (1992) *Fortress Europe: The meaning of 1992* London, Runnymeade Trust

Gould, N (2004) 'Qualitative research and social work: the methodological repertoire in a practice-orientated discipline' in Lovelock, R, Lyons, K and Powell, J (eds) *Reflecting on Social Work: Discipline and profession* Aldershot, Ashgate

Graham, M (2002) *Social Work and African-Centred Worldviews* Birmingham, Venture Press

Gustafson, P. (2002) 'Globalisation, multiculturalism and individualism' *Journal of Ethnic and Migration Studies*, 28(3), pp 463–81

Habermas, J. and Derrida, J. (2003) 'February 15, or what binds Europeans together: A plea for a common foreign policy, beginning in the core of Europe' *Constellations*, 10(3), pp 291–97, originally in the *Frankfurter Allgemeine Zeitung*, May 31 2003.

Hamburger, F (2003) *Einführung in die Sozialpädagogik* Stuttgart, Kohlhammer

Hamburger, F, Hirschler, S, Sander, D and Wöbcke, M (eds) (2004) *Ausbildung für Soziale Berufe in Europa* (Educating for Social Work in Europe) Frankfurt Am Main, ISS

Hansen, P (2004) 'In the name of Europe' *Race and Class*, 45(3), pp 49–62

Hantrais, L (1995) *Social Policy in the European Union* Houndsmills, Macmillan

Hantrais, L and Mangen, S (eds) (1996) *Cross National Research Methods in the Social Sciences* London, Pinter

Harder, M (1997) 'Child protection in Denmark' in Harder, M and Pringle, K *Protecting Children in Europe: Towards a new millennium* Aalborg, Aalborg University Press

Hart, E and Bond, M (eds.) (1995) *Action Research for Health and Social Care* Buckingham, Open University Press

Hatton, K (2001) 'Translating values: Making sense of different value bases – reflections from Denmark and the UK' *International Journal of Social Research Methodology*, 4(4), pp 265–78

Havrdova, Z (1998) 'Communication in international exchanges' in Chytil, O and Seibel, F (1999) *European Dimensions in Training and Practice of Social Professions* Albert, Ostrava, pp 203–13

Hazekamp, J L and Popple, K (eds) (1997) *Racism in Europe: A challenge for youth policy and youthwork* London, UCL Press

Healy, L (2001) *International Social Work: Professional action in an interdependent world* Oxford and New York, Oxford University Press

Held, D, McGrew, A, Goldblatt, D and Perraton, J. (1999) *Global Transformations: Politics, economics and culture*, Cambridge, Polity Press

Hering, S and Waaldkjk, B. (eds) (2003) *History of Social Work in Europe (1900 – 1960): Female pioneers and their influence on the development of international social organizations* Opladen, Leske and Budrich

Hetherington, R (1998) 'Issues in European child protection research' *European Journal of Social Work*, 1(1), pp 71–82

Higham, P (2001) 'Changing practice and an emerging social pedagogue paradigm in England: The role of the personal adviser' *Social Work in Europe*, 8(1), pp 21–28

Horncastle, J and Brobeck, H (1995) 'An international perspective on practice teaching for foreign students' *Social Work in Europe*, 2(3), pp 48–52

Horwath, J and Shardlow, S (2000) 'To interpret or translate? That is the question' *Social Work in Europe*, 7(2), pp 36–40

Hugman, R (1994) *Ageing and the Care of Older People in Europe* Basingstoke, Macmillan Press

Hume, S, Bevenuti, P, Gristina, D A and Reige, M (1998) 'Paradox in professional practice – women's views of social work: A tri-national study of England, Germany and Italy' *European Journal of Social Work*, 1(1), pp 55–70

Humphries, B (1999) 'Feminist evaluation' in Shaw, I and Lishman, J (eds) *Evaluation and Social Work Practice*, London, Sage Publications

Humphries, B. (2002) 'From welfare to authoritarianism: the role of social work in immigration controls' in Cohen, S, Humphries, B and Mynott, E (eds) *From Immigration Controls to Welfare Controls*, London, Routledge

Humphries, B (2004) 'Taking sides: social work research as a moral and political activity' in Lovelock, R, Lyons, K and Powell, J (eds) *Reflecting on Social Work: Discipline and profession*, Aldershot, Ashgate, pp 113–29

IASSW (International Association of Schools of Social Work) (2005) 'Global standards for social work education and training for social work professions', www.iassw-aiets.org, accessed 18/08/05

Ife, J (2001) 'Local and global practice: Relocating social work as a human rights profession in the new global order', *European Journal of Social Work*, 4(1), pp 5–16

IFSW (International Federation of Social Workers) (2004) 'Policy statement on globalisation and the environment', www.ifsw.org

Jacobsson, G (1998) 'Erasmus Evaluation of the Social Professions in Finland' in Lorenz, W and Seibel, F W (eds) *Erasmus Evaluation Conference: Social professions for a Social Europe*, National Reports, Koblenz, ECCE (CD-ROM)

Jean-Baptiste, A (2001) 'Africentric social work' in Dominelli, L, Lorenz, W and Haluk, S (eds) *Beyond Racial Divides: Ethnicities in social work* Aldershot Ashgate

Jovelin, E and Tully, E (2000) 'Social protection and social work in France' in Adams, A, Erath, P and Shardlow, S (eds) *Fundamentals of Social Work in Selected European Countries: Historical and political context, present theory, practice, perspectives* Lyme Regis, Russell House Publishing, pp 37–48

Juliusdottir, S and Petersson, J (2004) 'Nordic standards revisited', *Social Work Education*, 23(5), pp 567–80

Juntunen, E K and Hämäläinen, J (2001) 'Social care service and social work shaped by globalisation: example of Finland', Paper presented to the Inter-University Symposium: 'Globalisation and Small Countries', Dubrovnik, Croatia, 6 January

Kaletsky, A (2004) 'France's vision is not ours', *The Times*, 18 November

Karvinen, S (2003a) Speech at conference: Researching Social Work Practices, to celebrate the opening of the Helsinki 'Competence Centre', Helsinki, 10 January

Karvinen, S (2003b) 'Social work research developments in Finland', Presentation to CERTS seminar, Paris, 2 March

Karvinen, S, Pösö, T and Satka, M (eds) (1999) *Reconstructing Social Work Research: Finnish methodological adaptations* Jyvaskula, SoPhi, University of Jyvaskula

King, M (2004) 'Not what I had expected' *Professional Social Work*, July, pp 14–15

Kleinman, M (2002) *A European Welfare State?* Basingstoke, Palgrave

Köhnen, H (1992) *Deutsch-englisches Glossar der Jugendhilfe* Weinheim, Juventa

Kornbeck, J (ed) (2003) *Language Teaching in the Social Work Curriculum* Mainz, Logophon

Kornbeck, J (2004) 'Linguistic affinity and achieved geographical mobility: Evidence from the recognition of non-national qualifications in Ireland and the UK' *European Journal of Social Work*, 7(2) pp 143–66

Kristensen, S (2001) 'Learning by leaving: Towards a pedagogy for transnational mobility in the context of vocational education and training' *European Journal of Education*, 36(4), pp 412–30

Kronen, H (1986) 'Das Auftauchen des Terminus Sozialpädagogik' in Kanz, H (ed) *Bildungsgeschichte als Sozialgeschichte, Festschrift zum 60. Geburtstag von Franz Pöggeler* Frankfurt, Lang, pp 72–96

Krzyszkowski, J (2003) 'Social care and social work in Poland since 1989: Evidence for recent research, *Social Work in Europe*, 10(3) pp 71–5

Laot, F (2000) 'Doctoral work in the social work field in Europe' *Social Work in Europe*, 7(2), pp 2–7

Laot, F (2004) 'Stimulating a European research milieu in the field of social work' *European Journal of Social Work*, 7(2), pp 229–35

Lavenex, S (2001) 'Europeanization of refugee policies' *Journal of Common Market Studies*, 39(5), pp 851–74

Lawrence, S (2005) 'Symposium Report: International mobility of labour in social work: support and training implications, *European Journal of Social Work*, 8(2), pp 210–2

Lawrence, S and Reverda, N (1998) 'The development of the MACESS postgraduate programme for the social professions in Europe: The Hogeschool Maastricht/University of North London experience' *Social Work in Europe*, 5(3), pp 12–19

Lawrence, S and Reverda, N (2000) 'The recognition, evaluation and accreditation of European postgraduate programmes' *Social Work in Europe*, 7(2), pp 33–5

Leonard, M (1998) *Europe: The search for European identity* London, Demos, www.demos.co.uk

Lepalczyk, I and Marynowicz-Hetka, E (2001) 'Helena Radlinska (1879–1954) – Poland, a portrait of the person, researcher, teacher and social activist' *European Journal of Social Work*, 4(2), pp 191–6

Lewis, G (2000) 'Expanding the social policy imagery' in Lewis, G, Gewirtz, S, and Clarke, J (eds) *Rethinking Social Policy* London, Sage Publications/Oxford University Press, pp 1–21

Leibfried, S and Pierson, P (eds) (1995) *European Social Policy: Between fragmentation and integration* Washington, DC, Brookings Institution

Llobera, J (2001) 'What unites Europeans?' in Guibernau, M (ed) *Governing European Diversity* London, Sage Publications, pp 169–94

Lorenz, W (1994) *Social Work in a Changing Europe* London, Routledge

Lorenz, W (1998) 'Erasmus evaluation: The experience of the social professions' in Seibel F and Lorenz W (eds) *Social Professions for a Social Europe* Frankfurt, IKO-Verlag fur Interkulturelle Kommunikation, pp 121–53

Lorenz, W (1999) 'The ECSPRESS approach – guiding the social professions between national and global perspectives' in Chytil, O and Seibel, F W (eds) *European Dimensions and Training and Practice of Social Professions*, Erasmus TNP Conference Ostrava, Czechoslovakia, 28–31 August 1998, Boscovice, Albert, pp 13–28

Lorenz, W (2002) 'The social professions in Europe' *European Journal of Social Education*, no 3, pp 5–14

Lorenz, W (2003) 'European experiences in teaching social work' *Social Work Education*, 22(1), pp 7–18

Lorenz, W and Seibel, F. W (eds) (1998) Erasmus Evaluation Conference: *'Social Professions for a Social Europe'* Koblenz, ECCE (CD-ROM)

Lorenz, W and Seibel, F.W (1999) 'European educational exchanges in the social professions, the ECSPRESS experience' in Marynowicz-Hetka, E, Wagner, A and Piekarski, J (eds) *European Dimensions in Training and Practice of the Social Professions* (Dimensions Européennes de la formation et de la pratique des professions socials) Katowice, Slask, pp 315–41

Lorenz, W, Aluffi Pentini, A and Kniephoff, A (1998) 'Erasmus evaluation: The experience of the social professions, European Report' in Seibel, F W and Lorenz, W (eds) *Social Professions for a Social Europe* Frankfurt, IKO, pp 121–53

Lovelock, R, Lyons, K and Powell, J (eds) (2004) *Reflecting on Social Work: Discipline and profession* Aldershot, Ashgate

Lyons, K (1998) 'European dimensions in the training of the social professions Synthesis report' in Chytil, O and Seibel, F W (1999) *European Dimensions in Training and Practice of Social Professions* Blansko, Albert, pp 34–66

Lyons, K. (1999a) International Social Work: Themes and perspectives, Aldershot, Ashgate

Lyons, K (1999b) Social Work in Higher Education: Demise or development? Aldershot, Ashgate

Lyons, K (1999c) 'European dimensions in the training of social professions' in Chytil, O and Seibel, F (eds) European Dimensions in Training and Practice of the Social Professions, Blansko, Albert

Lyons, K (2000) Mapping Social Work Education: British element of IASSW global survey, Unpublished report to IASSW, JUC SWEC and CCETSW

Lyons, K (2002) 'Researching social work: Doctoral work in the UK' Social Work Education, 21(3), pp 337–46

Lyons, K (2003) 'Doctoral studies in social work: Exploring European developments' Social Work Education, 22(6), pp 555–64

Lyons, K (2004) 'Education for the social professions in the UK' in Hamburger, F, Hirschler, S, Sander, G and Wobke, M (eds) Ausbildung für Soziale Berufe in Europa, Frankfurt am Main, ISS

Lyons, K and Taylor, I (2004) 'Gender, knowledge and social work' in Lovelock, R, Lyons, K and Powell, J (eds) Reflecting on social work: Discipline and profession Aldershot, Ashgate, pp 72–94

Lyons, K, Manion, K and Carlsen, M (forthcoming) International Perspectives in Social Work: Local practice in global conditions Basingstoke, Palgrave

MacPherson Report (1999) Inquiry into the Murder of Stephen Lawrence London, Office of Public Sector Information

Manion, K (2002) 'Trafficking in women and children for sexual purposes: A growing threat in Europe' Social Work in Europe, 9(2), pp 14–22

Marynowicz-Hetka, E (1999) 'Dimensions Européennes dans la formation e la pratique des professions sociales' in Marynowicz-Hetka, E, Wagner, A and Piekarski, J (eds) European Dimensions in Training and Practice of the Social Professions (Dimensions Européennes de la formation et de la pratique des professions socials) Katowice, Slask, pp 397–408

Mason, T (2004) 'Denmark' in Campanini, A and Frost, E (eds) European Social Work: Commonalities and differences Rome, Carocci, pp 45–52

Masters, S (2003) 'On the other side' Professional Social Work, August, pp 16–17

May, T (2001) Social Research: Issues, methods and process Buckingham, Open University Press

McNay, M (1994) 'European social work: a degree' Social Work in Europe, 1(2), pp 15–17

Michie, J (ed) (2003) The Handbook of Globalisation, Cheltenham, Edward Elgar

Midgley, J (2000) 'Globalisation, capitalism and social welfare' Canadian Social Work Review, Special Issue, 2(1), pp 13–28

Milner, S (1998) 'Training policy: Steering between divergent national logics' in Hine, D and Kassim, H (eds) *Beyond the Market: The EU and national social policy*, London, Routledge, pp 156–77

Milward, A (2002) 'Historical teleologies' in Farrell, M, Fella, S and Newman, M (eds) *European Integration in the 21st Century* London, Sage Publications, pp 15–28

Mishra, R (1999) *Globalization and the Welfare State* Cheltenham, Edward Elgar

Modelski G (1972) *Principles of World Politics* New York, Free Press

Müller, K (2002) 'From the state to the market? Pension reform paths in Central-Eastern Europe' *Social Policy and Administration*, 36(2), pp 156–75

Munday, B (ed) (1989) *The Crisis in Welfare: An international perspective on social services and social work* Hemel Hempstead, Harvester Wheatsheaf

Murphy, M (2003) 'Covert action? Education, social policy and law in the European Union' *Journal of Education Policy*, 18(5), pp 551–62

Mynott, E and Humphries, B (2002) 'Young separated refugees: UK practice and Europeanisation' *Social Work in Europe*, 9(1), pp 18–27

Niemeyer, C (1998) *Klassiker der Sozialpädagogik – Einführung in die Theoriegeschichte einer Wissenschaft* Weinheim, Juventa

Nóvoa, A (2001) 'The restructuring of the European educational space: changing relationships among states, citizens and educational communities' in Fink, J, Lewis, G and Clarke, J (eds) *Rethinking European Welfare* London, Sage Publications, pp 249–75

O'Connell, P. (1999) *Astonishing Success: Economic growth and the labour market in Ireland*, Employment and Training Paper 44, International Labour Organisation, Geneva

OECD (Organisation for Economic Co-operation and Development) (2002) *Public Social Expenditure by Main Category as a Percentage of GDP (1980–1998)*, 6 May, Paris, OECD, www.oecd.org

Okitikpi, T and Aymer, K (2000) 'The price of safety: Refugee children and the challenge for social work' *Social Work in Europe*, 7(1), pp 51–8

Otto, H-U (2004) 'BA/MA – Neue Studienabschlüsse für den Bereich der Sozialen Arbeit im Wettbewerb der Moderne – Ausweg oder Irrweg?' in Steinmetz, B, Elsen, S and Seibel, F W (eds) *Der Bologna-Prozess in Europa, eine Herausforderung für die Ausbildung in der Sozialen Arbeit in Deutschland* Weimar, Bertuch, pp 55–62

Otto, H-U and Lorenz, W (1998) 'Editorial: The new Journal for the Social Professions in Europe' *European Journal of Social Work*, 1(1), pp 1–4

Patterson, E. (2004) 'Impact of globalisation in social work practice in Romania' in Tan, N-T and Rowlands, A (eds) *Social Work Around the World* Berne, International Federation of Social Workers

Pécseli, B. (1996) *Kultur & pædagogik*, København, Munksgaard/Rosinante

Pešič, V and Jovanovič, S (1986) 'Social work in Yugoslavia' in Brauns, H J and Kramer, D (eds) (1986) Social Work Education in Europe: A comprehensive description of social work education in 21 European countries Frankfurt, Eigenverlag des Deutschen Vereins für öffentliche und private Fürsorge, pp 557–73

Petrie, P (2003) 'Coming to terms with 'pedagogy': reconceptualising work with children' in Littlechild, B and Lyons, K (eds) Locating the Occupational Space for Social Work: International perspectives London, BASW/Venture Press, pp 11–16

Petrie, P (2004) Briefing Paper: Pedagogy – a holistic, personal approach to work with children and young people, across services: European models for practice, training, education and qualification London, Thomas Coram Research Unit, Institute of Education, University of London

Pfaffenberger, H (2004) 'Die Sozialarbeiter/Sozialpädagogen-Ausbildung und das neue Graduierungssystem' in Steinmetz, B, Elsen, S and Seibel, F W (eds) Der Bologna-Prozess in Europa, eine Herausforderung für die Ausbildung in der Sozialen Arbeit in Deutschland Weimar, Bertuch, pp 63–72

Pik, K. (1999) 'Problems in social work practice' in Marynowicz-Hetka, E, Wagner, A and Piekarski, J (eds) European Dimensions in Training and Practice of the Social Professions (Dimensions Europèennes de la formation et de la pratique des professions socials) Katowice, Slask, pp 161–84

Powell, J (2002) 'The changing conditions of social work research' British Journal of Social Work, 32(1), pp 17–33

Pringle, K (1998) Children and Social Welfare in Europe Buckingham, Open University Press

Prins, K (2004) 'Problem Based Project Work', Written communication with author

Prior, P and Sykes, R (2001) 'Evaluating theories and evidence' in Sykes, R, Palier, B and Prior, P (eds) Globalization and European Welfare States Basingstoke, Palgrave

Ramanathan, C and Link, R (eds) (1999) All our Futures: Principles and resources for global practice in a global era Carmel, LA, Brookes Cole

Rasmussen, T (2000) 'Thinking of the implementation of social work research: Different views from different epistemological approaches', Paper presented to the 2nd European Seminar, ETSUP, Paris, December

Rauschenbach, T (1999) Das sozialpädagogische Jahrhundert: Analysen zur Entwicklung sozialer Arbeit in der Moderne Weinheim, Juvent.

Reason, P and Bradbury, H (eds) (2001) Handbook of Action Research: Participative inquiry and practice London, Sage Publications.

Reverda, N (2001) 'The role of the personal adviser: Some observations on social pedagogy from the Netherlands' Social Work in Europe, 8(1), pp 29–30

Reverda, N and Richardson, J (2000) 'Watching the detectives: Reflections on dissertations of MACESS students' *Social Work in Europe*, 7(3), pp 1–7

Richards, H (1997) 'Global theatre' *Times Higher Education Supplement*, 7 February

Richardson, J and Lawrence, S (2005) 'European post-graduate education and research: theorising from course development' in Lyons, K and Littlechild, B (eds) *Internationalising Social Work Education: Considerations and developments* Birmingham, BASW/Venture Press

Ritchie, T (2004) *Relationer I teori og praksis* Copenhagen, Billeso and Baltzer

Robinson, L (1998) *'Race', Communication and the Caring Professions* Buckingham, Open University Press

Robinson, M. (2000) 'Human rights', Speech to the European Conference on Anti-Racism in the Preparation for the World Conference in Durban, Vienna, June

Room, G. (2002) 'Education and welfare: Recalibrating the European debate' *Policy Studies*, 23(1), pp 37–50

Ross, G (1995) *Jacques Delors and European Integration* Cambridge, Polity Press

Sakina Mama, R (2001) 'Preparing social work students to work in culturally diverse settings' *Social Work Education*, 20(3), pp 373– 82

Sanders, M (2003) 'Working with interpreters in personal social services' in Kornbeck, J (ed) *Language Teaching in the Social Work Curriculum* Mainz, Logophon

Satka, M and Karvinen, S (1999) 'The contemporary reconstruction of Finnish social work expertise' *European Journal of Social Work*, 2(2), pp 119–30

Scharpf, F (2002) 'The European Social Model: Coping with the challenges of diversity' *Journal of Common Market Studies*, 40(4), pp 645–70

Schneider, S (ed) (2003) *German Growth Potential: Facing the demographic challenge* Deutsche Bank Research (http://grupo.deutsche-bank.es/pdf/Informe_germangrowth_031215.pdf)

SCIE (Social Care Institute for Excellence (2003) *Knowledge Review 3: Types and quality of knowledge in social care*, London, SCIE, www.scie.org.uk

Sears, M and Brobeck, H (2003) 'Partnership Programme, BA European Social Work', Unpublished paper, University of Portsmouth

Seibel, F W (2004) 'Bologna docet' in Steinmetz, B, Elsen, S and Seibel, F W (eds) *Der Bologna-Prozess in Europa, eine Herausforderung für die Ausbildung in der Sozialen Arbeit in Deutschland* Weimar, Bertuch, pp 19–25

Seibel, F and Lorenz, W (eds) (1998) *Social Professions for a Social Europe* Proceedings of the Erasmus Evaluation Conference, Koblenz, 1996, Frankfurt, IKO.

Sewpaul, V and Jones, D (2004) 'Global standards for social work education and training' *Social Work Education*, 23(5), pp 493–513

Shardlow, S and Payne, M. (eds) (1997) *Contemporary Issues in Social Work: Western Europe* Aldershot, Arena

Shardlow, S M and Walliss, J (2003) 'Mapping comparative empirical studies of European social work' *British Journal of Social Work*, 33, pp 921–41

Shaw, I (2003) 'Cutting edge issues in social work research, critical commentary' *British Journal of Social Work*, 33, pp 107–16

Shore, C. (2000) *Building Europe* London, Routledge

Sims, J (2004) 'Fitting the bill', *Care and Health*, 18–24 May, p 23

Socrates (2002) *Socrates: Gateway to Education* Luxembourg: EC Directorate-General for Education and Culture, www.europa.int

Soydan, H. (2001) 'From vocational to knowledge-based education: An account of Swedish social work education' *Social Work Education*, 20(1), pp 111–21

Sünker, H and Otto, H-U (eds) (1997) *Education and Fascism* Bristol, Falmer Press

Taylor, Z (1999) 'Values, theories and methods in social work education: A culturally transferable core?' *International Social Work*, 42(3), pp 309–318

Taylor-Gooby, P (2001) *Welfare States under Pressure* London, Sage Publications

Teeple, G. (2000) *Globalization and the Decline of Social Reform: Into the 21st century* (2nd edition) Aurora, Ontario, Garamond Press

Threlfall, M. (2002) 'Social integration in the EU' in Farrell, M, Fella, S and Newman, M (eds) *European Integration in the 21st Century*, London, Sage Publications, pp 135–57

Threlfall, M. (2003) 'European social integration' *Journal of European Social Policy*, 13(2), pp 121–39

Thyer, B (2000) 'Developing discipline specific knowledge for social work – is it possible?', Paper presented to the IASSW Congress, Montreal, August

Toynbee, P. (2002) 'We need a fortress' *The Guardian*, 21 June 21

Trevillion, S. (1997) 'The globalisation of European Social Work', *Social Work in Europe*, 4(1), pp 1–9

Tsakloglou, P and Papadopoulos, F (2002) 'Aggregate level and determining factors of social exclusion in twelve European countries' *Journal of European Social Policy*, 12(3), pp 211–25

Urponen, K. (2004) 'Finland' in Campanini, A and Frost, E (eds) *European Social Work: Commonalities and differences* Rome, Carocci, pp 71–7

van der Laan, G (1998) 'The professional role of social work in a market environment' *European Journal of Social Work*, 1(1), pp 31–40

Van Der Wende, M (2001) 'The international dimension in national higher education policies: What has changed in Europe in the last five years' *European Journal of Education*, 36(4), pp 431–41

Vladinska, N. (2001) 'Country note: Bulgaria' *European Journal of Social Work* 4(1), pp 75–9

Walker, A and Maltby, T (1997) *Ageing Europe* Buckingham, Open University Press

Wallimann, I (2004) 'Bologna und GATS: zu erwartende Auswirkungen für den Hochschulraum' in Steinmetz, B, Elsen, S and Seibel, F W (eds) *Der Bologna-Prozess in Europa, eine Herausforderung für die Ausbildung in der Sozialen Arbeit in Deutschland* Weimar, Bertuch, pp 51–4

Webb, S (2004) 'Local orders and global chaos in social work', *European Journal of Social Work*, 6(2), pp 191–204

Weytes, A (2003) 'The challenges of comparative research' *Social Work in Europe*, 10(1), pp 1–8

Wilford, G (1997) 'One story – different perspectives: Users of childcare services in England and Germany' *Social Work in Europe*, 4(1), pp 23–31

Wilson, E (2004) 'Planning a mental health research project in Bulgaria', Presentation to the Social Work Research Seminar, University of East London, 11 February.

Written Communication and conversations with Christian Albro and Karen Prins, lecturers at Frobelseminariet, 2004

Yip, K-S (2004) 'A Chinese cultural critique of the global qualifying standards for education', *Social Work Education*, 23(5), pp 597–612

Young, I M (2003) *Europe and the global south: Towards a circle of equality* Open Democracy, 20 August, www.openDemocracy.net

Young, R (1996) *Intercultural Communication: Pragmatics, geneology, deconstruction* Philadelphia, Multilingual Matters Ltd

Websites

http://europa.eu.int/comm/education/programmes/mundus/call/call05_en.pdf, accessed 21/07/04

http://www.europarl.eu.int/comparl/libe/elsj/scoreboard/drugs/default_en.ht, accessed 18/03/05

www.certs-europe.com, accessed 28/04/04

www.coe.int/T/e/Com/about_coe/ (2004) *Membership and Purposes*, accessed 21/07/04

www.iassw-aiets.org, accessed 18/08/05

www.ifsw.org (2004) *The Ethics of Social Work – Principles and Standards*, accessed 17/08/05

www.magna-charta.org/home.html, accessed 28/04/04

www.mapping-the-way-forward.net/news.html, accessed 17/03/04